Nelson

ENGLISH

DEVELOPMENT

BOOK 4

JOHN JACKMAN
WENDY WREN

Nelson

Contents

Writing	Working with words
newspaper reports – front page story imaginative and descriptive Personal choice – personal experience/acrostic poem/diary	alliteration
first person narrative imaginative and descriptive Personal choice – research/interview/imaginative	figurative language
narrative research – travel brochure Personal choice – personal experience/acrostic poem/shape poem	looking at languages – French
playscript Personal choice – research/story ending/newspaper report	figurative language
factual accounts paragraphs Personal choice – imaginative description/personal letter	looking at languages – Greek
personal experience advantages/disadvantages imaginative Personal choice – imaginative description/personal experience/interview	using a thesaurus
imaginative personal experience graph Personal choice – diary/horoscope/opinion	figurative language
science fiction stories conversation Personal choice – opinion/newspaper report/research	descriptive language using a thesaurus
diaries Personal choice – personal letter/opinion	optimism – optimistic (word family 'istic')
paragraphs report interviews Personal choice – imaginative description/research	naturalist (word family 'ist')
adventure stories – purpose and audience Personal choice – research/personal letter	proverbs
magazine articles purpose and audience Personal choice – conversation/diary/research	telegram (word family 'tele')
book blurbs Personal choice – imaginative description/research/book blurbs	new words

Flood!

In most cultures there is a story of a flood. This is the story of Noah and the flood that is told in the Book of Genesis in the Bible.

People robbed and killed each other and were so wicked that God felt sorry that he had ever made human beings who treated one another so badly. He was angry at the wrong he saw. At last there was only one man left who still loved God and followed his ways. His name was Noah.

So God warned Noah, 'People are so cruel that they are destroying one another and my beautiful world. I am going to send lots of rain. All the lakes and rivers, even the sea itself, will overflow and rush over the earth, until every living thing has been drowned in the flood. I promise I shall keep you and your family safe.' God continued, 'You must build a boat . . .'

God told Noah exactly how the boat was to be made. It was to be built of a special kind of wood and was to have three decks. The whole boat was to be 150 metres long and it was to be coated inside and outside with tar.

Noah obeyed God's instructions and his family helped him. Every day astonished crowds watched them as they cut down trees and smoothed the wood. The bystanders jeered. 'Noah is mad,' they said. 'There is no water here to float a ship!'

Noah took not the slightest notice. Then God told him to drive into the boat two of every kind of animal, bird and reptile. So Noah and his family rounded up the animals and drove them in. Two by two, one male and one female – all had to be aboard before the rain came.

When the animals were safely settled in the boat Noah and his family went aboard too. They took a last look at the old world. Then God himself shut the door behind them.

There was a flash of lightning and a crash of thunder. The dark swollen clouds that filled the sky burst and it began to rain. Water poured down the hills and, filling the valleys, rose higher and higher. The big boat jolted and began to drift, gently floating on the flood.

Everywhere people tried to escape. Faster and faster rose the boat on the foaming swirling water until it was tossed high above the tops of the highest mountains. Every living thing on earth drowned as the sea covered the whole world.

Inside, Noah and his company were crowded and a bit cramped. The family was busy from morning until night cleaning the pens, changing the straw, bringing food and water to the animals.

For forty days and forty nights the sound of rain continued overhead. But God did not forget Noah and the animals in the boat. At last the rain died away and a wind blew over the flooded world. Slowly the water went down until at last the boat came to rest on the top of a double-peaked mountain called Ararat.

The wind kept blowing. Soon the peaks of other mountains showed like rocks sticking out of the sea.

Noah opened a trap-door and looked out. He decided to send a raven out to investigate. The bird gave a harsh croak and flew away. It never came back to the boat, but circled the flooded country looking for somewhere to rest. So a little later Noah sent out a dove.

Everyone gathered round to watch as the bird shook its white feathers and flew off, but it found nowhere to settle and came back to the boat. A week later Noah tried again. All day the family watched anxiously. Then in the evening the bird came back. Everyone cheered when they saw that the bird held an olive leaf in its beak. Soon they would be able to leave their boat and make a fresh start in God's new world.

At last the day came when God said to Noah, 'You may let the animals out now.' With a flurry of feathers and pounding of hooves they rushed out of the boat. Last of all Noah and his family stepped shakily off the boat. It was good to be alive in this clean new world.

Then God said to Noah, 'I will never send another flood to destroy the world. Until the end of time there will always be times to plant and times to harvest, hot weather and cold weather, day and night. Look, I am putting my bow in the sky so that you will remember my promise.'

Adapted from *The Ladybird Bible Story Book*

COMPREHENSION

1 Why do you think God warned Noah about the flood?
2 What does the writer mean by saying that Noah took a last look at 'the old world'?
3 Why do you think that the boat had to be coated with tar?
4 Why did the bystanders think that Noah was mad?
5 How do you think they felt when it began to rain?
6 Why were Noah and his family pleased to see the dove with an olive leaf in its beak?

1 Imagine you are a newspaper reporter and you are going to write a front page story about Noah building the boat.

2 Look at the diagram and read the notes opposite carefully. They will help you to plan your work.

NAME OF YOUR NEWSPAPER

Headline

Reporter's name

THE NEWSPAPER REPORT.

Blah blah blah blah blah blah blah-blah blah blah blah blah-blah blah blah blah blah-blah blah blah blah blah-blah blah blah blah blah-blah blah blah blah blah-blah blah blah blah blah-blah blah blah blah blah-blah blah blah blah blah

blah blah blah blah blah blah blah blah blah blah blah blah blah blah blah blah blah blah blah blah-blah blah blah blah blah-blah blah blah blah blah-blah blah blah blah blah-blah blah blah blah blah-blah blah blah blah blah-blah blah blah blah blah

blah blah blah blah blah blah blah blah blah blah blah blah blah blah blah-blah blah blah blah blah-blah blah blah blah blah-blah blah blah blah blah-blah blah blah blah blah-blah blah blah blah blah-blah blah blah blah blah-blah blah blah blah blah-blah blah blah blah blah

blah blah blah blah blah blah blah blah blah blah blah blah blah blah blah-blah blah blah blah blah-blah blah blah blah blah-blah blah blah blah blah-blah blah blah blah blah-blah blah blah blah blah-blah blah blah blah blah-blah blah blah blah blah

blah blah blah

blah blah blah blah blah blah blah blah blah blah blah blahblah blah blah blah blahblah blah blah blah blahblah blah blah blah blahblah blah blah blah blahblah blah blah

blah blahblah blah blah blah blahblah blah blah blah blahblah blah blah blah blahblah blah blah blah blahblah blah blah blah blah

blah blahblah blah blah blah blah blah blah blah blah blah blah blah blah blah blah blah blah blah blah blah blah blah blah blah blah blah blah blah blah blah blah blah blah blah blah blah blah blah blah blah blah blah blah blah blah blah blah blah blah blah blah blah blah blah

blah blah blah blah blah blah blah blah blah blah blah blah blah blah blah-blah blah blah blah blah-blah blah blah blah blah-blah blah blah blah blah-blah blah blah blah blah-blah blah blah blah blah-blah blah blah blah blah-blah blah blah blah blah-blah blah blah blah blah-blah blah blah blah blah

blah blah blah blah blah blah blah blah blah blah blah blah blah blahblah blah blah blah blah blahblah blah blah blah blah blahblah blah blah blah blah blah blah blah blah blah blah

ILLUSTRATION

Blah blah blah blah blah blah blah blah blah blah blah blah blahblah blah blah blah blahblah blah blah blah blahblah blah blah blah blah-blah blah blah blah blahblah blah blah blah blahblah blah blah blah blahblah blah blah blah blahblah blah blah blah blah blah

blah blah blah blah blah blah blah blah blah blah blah blah blah blahblah blah blah blah blah blahblah blah blah blah blah blah blah blah blah blah blah

blah blah blah blah blah blah blah blah blah blah blah blah blah blahblah blah blah blah blahblah blah blah blah blahblah blah blah blah blah blah

blah blah blah blah blah blah

blah blah blah blah blah blah blah blah blahblah blah blah blah blahblah blah blah blah blahblah blah blah blah blahblah blah blah blah blah

blah blah blah

blah blah blah blah blah blah blah blah blah blah blah blah-blah blah blah blah blahblah blah blah blah blahblah blah blah blah blahblah blahblah blah blah blah blah-blah blah blah blah blahblah blah blah blah blah

blah blah blah blah blah blah blah blah blah blah blah blah blah blahblah blah blah blah blahblah blah blah blah blahblah blah blah blah blahblah blah blah blah blah-blah blah blah blahblah blah blah blah blahblah blah blah blah blahblah blah blah blah blah blah

blah blah blah blah blah blah

Name of your newspaper

You can use the name of a newspaper that you already know or it might be more fun to make one up.

- How will you write the name?
- Will you print it or use fancy writing?
- If you are using a computer, what style of print will you use?

Headline

This is very important. If people find a headline interesting or amusing they will want to read the report. Just writing 'Noah builds a boat' will not 'grab' their attention. Think of a really clever headline for your story. You could use alliteration. (This is when two or more words start with the same sound.)

Reporter's name

In a newspaper, the name of the reporter/writer appears at the beginning of the story. This is called a by-line. Use your own name or make one up.

Illustration

A newspaper report is more interesting if there is a drawing or photograph to go with it. Sometimes the illustration shows one of the main people in the report. Sometimes it shows what is happening. Remember that your illustration should help the reader to understand the report.

The newspaper report

Your report should include:

- the facts – what actually happened. Read through the story of Noah again on pages 4 and 5. Remember that you are reporting on the building of the boat. (Why can't you write a report about the flood?)

- opinion – the way you write your report will show the reader what you think of Noah. Do you think he is a sensible man that your readers should take notice of? Or do you think he is crazy?

- eye-witness accounts – you can interview some of the 'bystanders' who jeered at Noah. Was there anyone in the crowd who thought he was doing the right thing? You could also interview some of Noah's family or Noah himself.

3 Try to make your finished piece of work look like the front page of a newspaper.

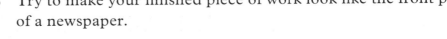

Noah

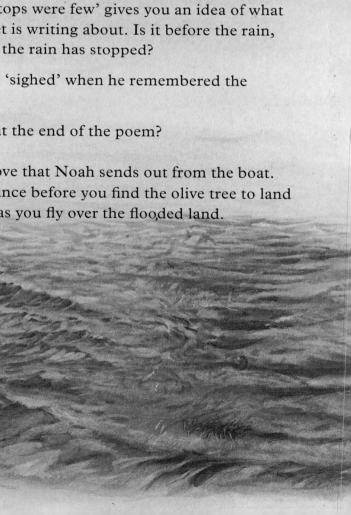

When old Noah stared across the floods,
Sky and water melted into one
Looking-glass of shifting tides and sun.

Mountain-tops were few: the ship was foul:
All the morn old Noah marvelled greatly
At this weltering world that shone so stately,
Drowning deep the rivers and the plains.
Through the stillness came a rippling breeze;
Noah sighed, remembering the green trees.

Clear along the morning stooped a bird, –
Lit beside him with a blossomed sprig.
Earth was saved; and Noah danced a jig.

Siegfried Sassoon

COMPREHENSION

Read the poem and answer the questions.

1 Why does the poet describe the sky and water as a 'looking-glass'?

2 The phrase 'Mountain-tops were few' gives you an idea of what part of the story the poet is writing about. Is it before the rain, during the rain, or after the rain has stopped?

3 Why do you think Noah 'sighed' when he remembered the 'green trees'?

4 How was Noah feeling at the end of the poem?

DESCRIPTIVE WRITING

Imagine that you are the dove that Noah sends out from the boat. You have to fly quite a distance before you find the olive tree to land on. Describe what you see as you fly over the flooded land.

Choose one of the following assignments:

1 Imagine you are Noah. Write diary entries for:
   - the day you sent out the raven
   - the first day you sent out the dove
   - the day you sent out the dove and it came back with the olive leaf.

   Remember to record what happened and how you felt about it.

2 Write an acrostic poem on a watery word. Here are some suggestions:

   flood   downpour   torrent

Acrostic means a poem or puzzle in which the first (or last) letters of each line spell a word.

3 Have you ever experienced a 'flood'? A burst pipe at home, a leaky roof? Do you live near a river which bursts its banks when there is heavy rain? Write about your own experience.

WORKING WITH WORDS

Round the **r**ugged **r**ock, the **r**agged **r**ascal **r**an.

Repeating the same sound at the beginning of two or more words is called **alliteration**. You will often see alliteration used for headlines in newspapers.

Heavy hailstorm hits Holt

Farmer's fields flooded in Farndon!

Record rainfall recorded

Make up headlines for these stories using alliteration.

1 A snowfall in June.

2 People having a picnic who are chased by a bull.

Shipwrecked!

*Robinson Crusoe, written in 1720 by Daniel Defoe, is the story of a young man
who runs away to sea and is shipwrecked. The passage tells of how he
survived the shipwreck and landed on a South Sea island. As this
was written over 200 years ago, the language and style seem
difficult. Read it once, then read it carefully again.*

Nothing can describe the confusion of thought which I
felt when I sunk into the water; for though I swam very
well, yet I could not deliver myself from the waves so
as to draw breath, till that wave having driven me,
or rather carried me, a vast way on towards the shore
and, having spent itself, went back, and left me
upon the land almost dry, but half dead with the
water I took in. I had so much presence of mind
as well as breath left, that seeing myself nearer
the mainland than I expected, I got upon my
feet, and endeavoured to make on towards
the land as fast as I could, before another
wave should return and take me up again.
But I soon found it was impossible to
avoid it . . .
The wave that came upon
me again, buried me at once twenty
or thirty feet deep in its own body; and I
could feel myself carried with a mighty force
and swiftness towards the shore a very great way;
but I held my breath and assisted myself to swim still
forward with all my might. I was ready to burst with
holding my breath, when, as I felt myself rising up, so,
to my immediate relief, I found my head and hands shoot
out above the surface of the water; and though it was not two
seconds of time that I could keep myself so, yet it relieved me
greatly, gave me breath and new courage. I was covered again
with water a good while, but not so long but I held it out; and
finding the water had spent itself and began to return, I struck
forward against the return of the waves, and felt ground again
with my feet. I stood still a few moments to recover breath, and
till the water went from me, and then took to my heels, and run
with what strength I had farther towards the shore. But neither would this
deliver me from the fury of the sea, which came pouring in after me again, and twice

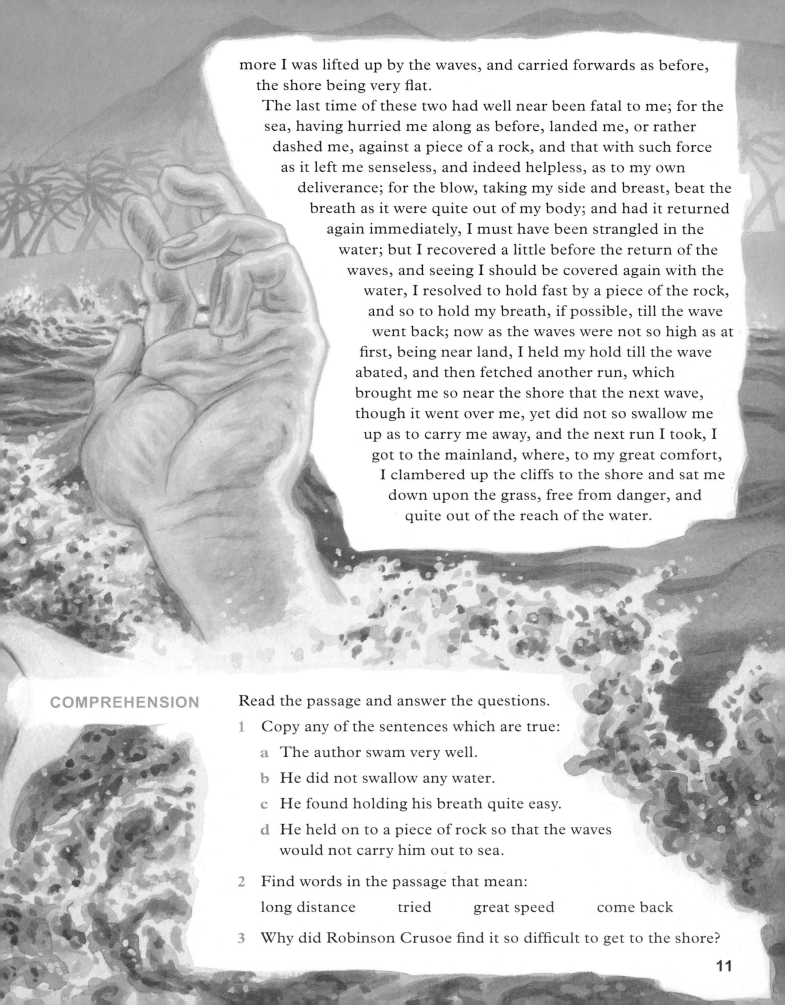

more I was lifted up by the waves, and carried forwards as before, the shore being very flat.

The last time of these two had well near been fatal to me; for the sea, having hurried me along as before, landed me, or rather dashed me, against a piece of a rock, and that with such force as it left me senseless, and indeed helpless, as to my own deliverance; for the blow, taking my side and breast, beat the breath as it were quite out of my body; and had it returned again immediately, I must have been strangled in the water; but I recovered a little before the return of the waves, and seeing I should be covered again with the water, I resolved to hold fast by a piece of the rock, and so to hold my breath, if possible, till the wave went back; now as the waves were not so high as at first, being near land, I held my hold till the wave abated, and then fetched another run, which brought me so near the shore that the next wave, though it went over me, yet did not so swallow me up as to carry me away, and the next run I took, I got to the mainland, where, to my great comfort, I clambered up the cliffs to the shore and sat me down upon the grass, free from danger, and quite out of the reach of the water.

COMPREHENSION

Read the passage and answer the questions.

1 Copy any of the sentences which are true:

 a The author swam very well.

 b He did not swallow any water.

 c He found holding his breath quite easy.

 d He held on to a piece of rock so that the waves would not carry him out to sea.

2 Find words in the passage that mean:

 long distance   tried   great speed   come back

3 Why did Robinson Crusoe find it so difficult to get to the shore?

Daniel Defoe wrote the story of *Robinson Crusoe* as if it had happened to him. He wrote it in the **first person**.

You write in the **first person** when:

- you are writing about something that actually happened to you
- you imagine that something has happened to you.

1 In the story, Robinson Crusoe tells us

a what happened:
'**I** could feel **myself** carried with a mighty force'
'**I** recovered a little before the return of the waves'

b what he felt like:
'half dead with the water **I** took in'
'**I** was ready to burst with holding **my** breath'

2 The problem with writing in the first person is that it can be very boring if you begin every sentence with **I**.

I went down to the sea early that morning. **I** looked at the ships. **I** noticed one of them was leaning to the side. **I** watched it sink lower and lower into the water. **I** saw it slip under the waves.

We can improve this piece of writing by changing the beginning of the sentences.

Early that morning I went down to the sea to look at the ships. I noticed one of them was leaning to the side. I watched it sink lower and lower into the water. I saw it slip under the waves.

We have improved it by changing the order of the words in the first sentence and joining two sentences together:

I went down to the sea **early that morning**.
Early that morning I went down to the sea to look at the ships.

▲ Improve these sentences by changing the order of the words.

a I like to watch the waves when I go to the seaside.

b I can go on a boat trip tomorrow if it doesn't rain.

c I like swimming although I'm not very good at it.

3 We can improve this piece of writing further by using conjunctions (joining more sentences together):

I noticed one of them was leaning to the side. I watched it sink lower and lower into the water. I saw it slip under the waves.

I noticed one of them was leaning to the side **and** I watched it sink lower and lower **until** it slipped under the waves.

▲ Improve these sentences by joining them together.

a I saw the spider. I ran out of the room.

b I went to the shops. I needed to buy some books.

c I found a ten pence piece under the bed. I wasn't looking for it.

▲ Rewrite the following and improve it by changing the beginning of the sentences and joining some sentences together.

I went swimming yesterday. I had been given goggles for my birthday. I wanted to try them out. I knew that the swimming pool opened at ten o'clock. I caught the half-past-nine bus. I was the first one there. I had the pool to myself for half an hour. I had a good swim. I really enjoyed myself.

4 Now imagine you are in the same situation as Robinson Crusoe but you can breathe easily under water. You don't try to get to the shore but sink to the bottom of the sea to have a look around.

Write about what you see. Remember:

● use the first person – **I** – as this is happening to you

● describe what happens

● describe how you feel

● think of interesting ways to begin your sentences – **don't** start with **I** all of the time.

'The Storm' by JMW Turner, British Museum, London © British Museum

This picture was painted by JMW Turner in 1823. He was very interested in painting the sea. Some of his pictures show calm, peaceful scenes and some, like this one, show the sea during a violent storm.

1   Look carefully at the picture and make a list of all the things you can see in it.

2   Make a list of the colours in the picture. Try to be as accurate as possible. Use a dictionary and thesaurus to help you.
   ● Look at each colour in turn.
   ● Are there different shades of any of the colours?
   ● How can you describe each shade?

3   Make some notes on how the picture makes you feel.
   ● Do you like it? Why?
   ● Do you dislike it? Why?
   ● How do you think Turner wanted his audience to feel when they looked at the picture?

4   Using your lists and notes, write a description of the picture. Imagine your description is for someone who has never seen a ship caught in a storm at sea.

Choose one or two of the following assignments:

1 Continue the story of Robinson Crusoe from where he climbed up the cliff to safety. Remember:

- You know the **setting** – an island. We are not told very much about it so you will have to make some notes about the sort of island it is. Is it uninhabited or do people live there? Is there a lot of vegetation or is it bare and rocky?

- You know one of the **characters** – Robinson Crusoe. Is there anyone else on the island? Does someone else come to the island?

- You know the **plot** so far – Robinson Crusoe has been shipwrecked on the island. What is going to happen next? How will you **end** the story?

2 Imagine Robinson Crusoe is rescued two weeks after being shipwrecked on the island. You are going to interview him for your local newspaper. Make a list of questions you would ask him.

3 Using encyclopedias and reference books, find out about JMW Turner. Ask your teacher for a photocopy of a Fact File sheet to record the information you find.

WORKING WITH WORDS

Look at these **watery** expressions.
Write out the correct meaning in your book.

1 If you swallow something **hook, line and sinker**, do you:

 a believe everything someone tells you?
 b have a fishing rod for your tea?

2 If you are determined to do something even if you **sink or swim**, are you:

 a sure you will succeed?
 b not sure how it will turn out?

3 If you are said to be **in hot water**, are you:

 a having a very hot bath?
 b in trouble?

4 If you are **between the devil and the deep blue sea**, are you:

 a in a very difficult position?
 b a bad person going for a swim?

Paris

The Seine is the river which runs through Paris. It has been painted by many artists in all seasons.

'The Seine at Argenteuil' by Edouard Manet
Private Collection (on loan to the Courtauld Institute Galleries, London)

PICTURE STUDY

Look at Manet's painting and answer the questions.

1   What are the two main colours the artist has used?

2   How do the colours make you feel?

3   Say what you like and dislike about the picture.

4   Make a Fact File on Edouard Manet.

A SETTING FOR A STORY

Look again at the painting by Manet. There is a lady with a child by the side of the river. Use this setting and these characters to write a story.

1 Things to think about:

- **Who are the characters?**
  What are their names?
  What is their relationship?

- **Where have they come from?**
  Do they live nearby?
  Are they visiting?

- **Why are they by the river?**
  Are they meeting someone?
  Are they lost?

- **What is going to happen?**
  Work out the plot and the ending before you begin to write.

- **How will you begin?**
  Will you begin with a conversation between the two characters?
  Will you begin by describing the setting?

- **How do you want your reader to feel?**
  Is it a sad story?
  Will it have a happy ending?
  Will the reader feel frightened, amused, puzzled, or scared?

- **Who is your audience?**
  Are you writing for younger people?
  Are you writing for people who like mysteries?
  Are you writing for people who like adventure?

2 Make notes on all the things above.
  Work out what is going to happen in each paragraph.

3 Think of an interesting title for your story.

4 Write your story.

A TRIP TO PARIS

Paris is the capital city of France. Many tourists go there as there are many different things to see.

You are going to write an article for a travel brochure to encourage people to visit Paris. You will need to:

- find out information about the various things that you can see in Paris.
- choose your vocabulary carefully so that Paris sounds an interesting and exciting place to visit.

Here is how to plan your work.

1 Look at the photographs. Answer the questions by using reference books and encyclopedias. You do not have to write in full sentences. You are making notes to help you later on.

The Eiffel Tower

- When was it built?
- Who designed it?
- How high is it?
- How many steps has it?
- In what year was it nearly pulled down?
- How much does it weigh?

Notre Dame

- What is it?

- When did construction begin?

- When was construction complete?

- Who was King of France at the time?

- Who was crowned Emperor in it?

- What famous novel uses
  Notre Dame as its setting?

The Louvre

- What is it?

- What was it originally used for?

- What famous painting by
  Leonardo da Vinci is in the Louvre?

- When was it first opened to the public?

The Metro

- What is it?

- When did the people of Paris first use it?

- What other cities have a similar form of transport?

2 Try to find more information on Paris.
- Are there any other famous buildings?
- What can you find out about the River Seine?
- What particular food would you get in Paris?

3 When you have written your notes on all the things you are going to include in your brochure you need to plan what it will look like.

- Are you going to have one picture or several pictures?

- Are you going to arrange your writing so that it is all together or in paragraphs with each picture?

4 You now have to think carefully about how you are going to write up your notes. Which of these sentences is more likely to make you want to visit Notre Dame?

      Notre Dame is a cathedral in Paris.

or

      Notre Dame is a **magnificent** cathedral in the heart of the **exciting** city of Paris.

Both sentences give the same information but by adding the words **magnificent** and **exciting** it makes the reader much more interested. Write up your notes in paragraphs, choosing your words carefully.

5 Now do your drawings or use pictures cut from magazines. You might like to include a map of France to show where Paris is.

6 Read through your work carefully and check the following:
- spelling
- punctuation
- choice of words
- the purpose of this piece of writing is to persuade people to visit Paris. Do you think it does its job?

7 When you are satisfied that you have done the best piece of work you can, write it neatly.

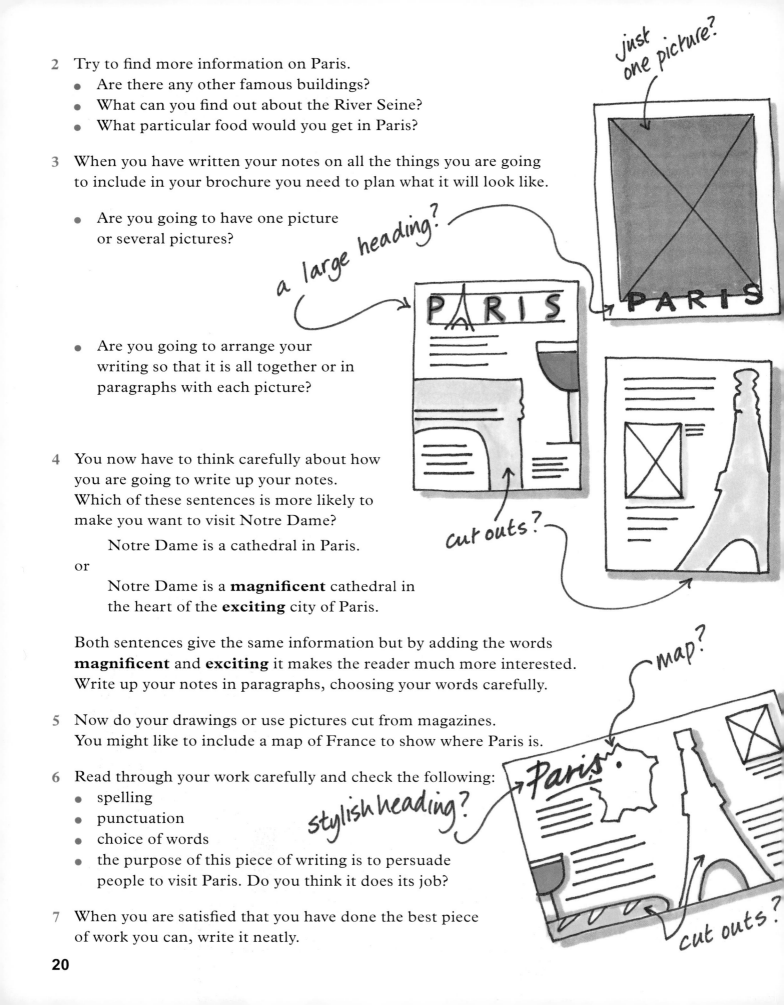

just one picture?

a large heading?

cut outs?

map?

stylish heading?

cut outs?

PERSONAL CHOICE   Choose one of the following assignments:

1   Have you ever been to France or any other country for a holiday? Write about what you saw there and what you did. The way you write it will tell your reader whether or not you enjoyed your holiday.

2   Write an acrostic poem or a shape poem for **one** of these words:

   Paris   river   tower

WORKING WITH WORDS   We have many words in English that have a near relation in French. Can you find near relations in English to these French words? The clues will help you.

French words	Clues
comprendre – to understand	You do this exercise at the beginning of each unit in Nelson English. (*Answer:* Comprehension)
rougir – to blush	Women use this as make-up.
dormir – to sleep	This is a room with lots of beds in it.
escalier – stairs	A moving staircase.
femme – woman	The opposite of masculine.
lune – moon	28 days is a _ _ _ _ _ month.
coucher – to lie down	Another word for a sofa or settee.
cygne – a swan	A baby swan.

Greek theatre

Plan of the theatre at Epidavros

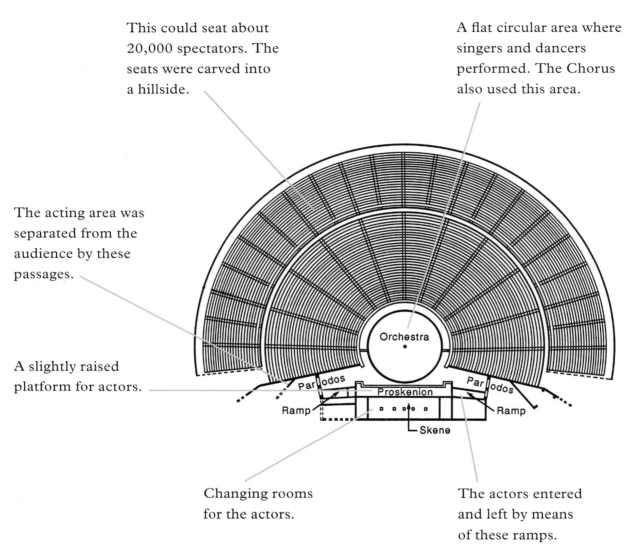

This could seat about 20,000 spectators. The seats were carved into a hillside.

A flat circular area where singers and dancers performed. The Chorus also used this area.

The acting area was separated from the audience by these passages.

A slightly raised platform for actors.

Changing rooms for the actors.

The actors entered and left by means of these ramps.

(Labels on diagram: Orchestra, Par odos, Par odos, Proskenion, Ramp, Ramp, Skene)

Greek theatre began as religious festivals in honour of the god Dionysus. Over the years plays were written about other heroes and gods as well.

The playscript had the words for each actor and for a group known as the Chorus who commented on the action. Any violence or death took place off-stage and the audience was kept informed of what was going on by a messenger character who came on-stage and reported what was happening.

The actors wore masks to show what sort of character they were. They wore platform shoes and padding so that the audience could see them from a long way off.

Epidavros as it is today

Read the passage and look carefully at the diagram to answer the questions.

1 What is the proskenion?

2 Where did the Chorus perform?

3 How did Greek theatre begin?

4 What was the role of the messenger?

5 What did the actors do to make sure they could be seen?

23

Read the story of the Greek hero Theseus.

Theseus's father Aegeus, King of Athens, had to send seven youths and seven maidens as a tribute to King Minos of Crete so that Athens would not be attacked. The young people were to be fed to the Minotaur, a monster who was half man, half beast and who lived in the centre of a complicated maze known as the Labyrinth.

When Theseus heard this he exclaimed, 'I will go myself as one of the young men, and meet the Minotaur!'

In vain Aegeus begged him not to be so foolhardy. 'If I slay the Minotaur,' said Theseus, 'it will surely save our country from further tribute – so go I will.'

'Then promise me,' said Aegeus sadly, 'that if you return victorious you will hoist white sails on your ship: but if you do not, the black sails that waft the Athenian youths and maidens to their doom will tell me that you have perished with them.'

Promising this, Theseus set out for Crete, and in due time arrived at Cnossus where the mighty Minos ruled. Here the victims were kindly entertained, and took part in racing and boxing contests before the king and his court. As Theseus stood panting at the winning post, the Princess Ariadne saw him and straightway loved him.

In great misery at the thought of the fate which awaited him, Ariadne at length thought of a scheme. That night she visited Theseus. 'Ask to go first into the Labyrinth tomorrow,' she instructed him. 'No one has ever found his way out again, but if you take with you this ball of thread, without it being discovered, and fasten one end to the door when it is closed after you, unrolling it as you go, you may find your way back by means of it. I will be at the door at midnight to let you out if you are successful; but you must take me with you in your flight, for it will not be safe here when it is known that I helped you.'

Theseus did exactly as he was told, and next day he entered the Labyrinth with the thread concealed in his hand. When alone, he attached one end to the lintel of the door, and unwound the thread behind him as he traced his way through the winding passages, leading up and down, hither and thither, until he came to the great chamber or cavern in the centre where the dim light from above showed the monster waiting for him.

The Minotaur was a fearsome creature with a great human body and the head and neck of a bull. Its skin was as tough as the toughest leather and a dull yellow colour like brass.

When it saw Theseus, it rushed upon him bellowing with rage and hunger.

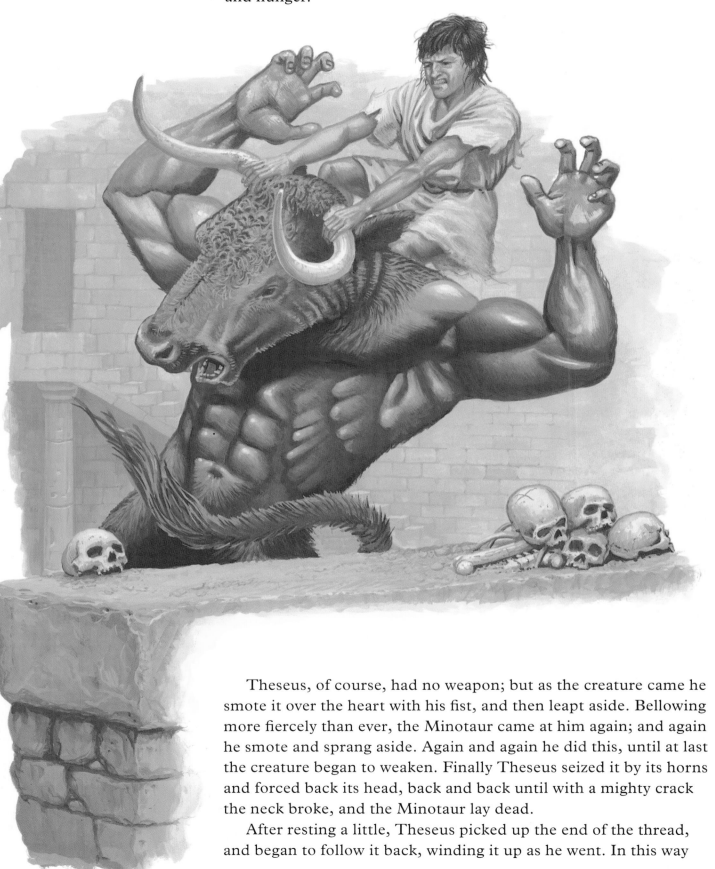

Theseus, of course, had no weapon; but as the creature came he smote it over the heart with his fist, and then leapt aside. Bellowing more fiercely than ever, the Minotaur came at him again; and again he smote and sprang aside. Again and again he did this, until at last the creature began to weaken. Finally Theseus seized it by its horns and forced back its head, back and back until with a mighty crack the neck broke, and the Minotaur lay dead.

After resting a little, Theseus picked up the end of the thread, and began to follow it back, winding it up as he went. In this way

he at length reached the door, where Ariadne was waiting for him. Swiftly she led him and the other intended victims to their ship; and while it was still dark they crept on board, cut the cables and stole silently away.

Adapted from *Tales of the Greek Heroes* by Roger Lancelyn Green

You are going to turn the story of Theseus and the Minotaur into a playscript. When you write a play you must include:

- the setting – **scene**
- the names of the people in the play – **characters**
- what the characters say – **dialogue**
- what the characters do – **stage directions**

1 **Scene and characters**

In this story there are many different settings so you will have to work out where and when things happen and which characters appear in each scene. Go through the story and set it out like this:

Scene	Setting	Characters
One	the palace at Athens	Theseus Aegeus
Two	on board ship	Theseus other victims sailors Captain

Now work out the other scenes and characters.

2 **Dialogue**

You will find some conversations in the story but you can make up some extra dialogue. Imagine how the characters feel and what they might say in the different scenes. What are the other victims talking about? What will Theseus say to Ariadne when she tells him her plan? What will Theseus say to himself when he sees the Minotaur for the first time?

3 **Stage directions**

You can work out the stage directions from what the characters do in the story, for example:

> Theseus enters the Labyrinth hiding the ball of thread in his hand.

Choose one or two of the following assignments:

1   Perseus and Heracles were both Greek heroes. Find out what you can about them and put the information in a Fact File.

2   Read the story of Theseus and the Minotaur again. How do you think the story ends? Did Theseus and Ariadne get away? Did King Minos send soldiers after them? Write an ending for the story.

3   Write a newspaper report about Theseus's adventure. Remember:
    • an interesting headline
    • illustrations
    • facts/opinions/interviews/eye-witness accounts.

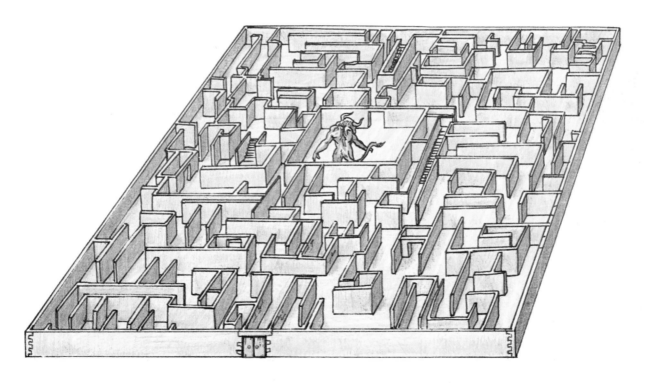

Theseus went **hither and thither** in the Labyrinth. This means he went here and there.

What does it mean when we say:

1   Everything is going to **rack and ruin**.

2   They fought **tooth and nail**.

3   The two runners were racing **neck and neck**.

4   To join the army you must be sound in **wind and limb**.

Can you think of any more?

The original Olympics

Read the information in the four books about sport in Ancient Greece and answer the questions.

Life in
ANCIENT GREECE

ANCIENT GREECE

In Ancient Greece there were many sports competitions but the four biggest ones were known as the Panhellenic Games.

People came from all over the Greek world to take part. Many buildings were erected for the Games. These were for competitors, important people who came to watch, and religious ceremonies. At Olympia there was a Temple of Zeus. The statue of the god was about 13 metres high and was one of the Seven Wonders of the Ancient World.

34

35

THE ANCIENT GREEKS

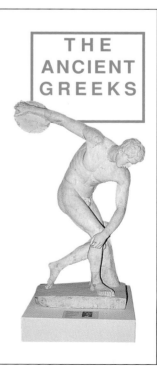

The Olympic Games were held in honour of the god Zeus. No one knows exactly when they began, but official records were kept from 776 BC. At first there was only one event, running, but others were added later, such as wrestling, boxing, chariot racing, horse racing and the pentathlon. The prizes were olive wreaths, palm branches and woollen ribbons. If any athlete had performed really well, a statue was put up in his honour.

2

3

The History of the Olympics

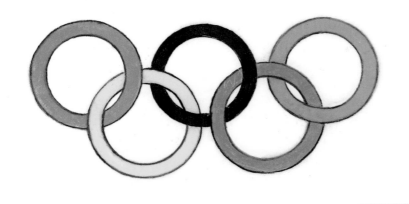

four

Of all the Panhellenic competitions, the Olympic Games were the most important. They were held every four years at Olympia and only lasted one day until the 77th Olympiad when this was extended to five days. Running, wrestling and boxing took place in the Stadium. Chariot and horse racing were held in the Hippodrome.

five

PEOPLES OF THE PAST

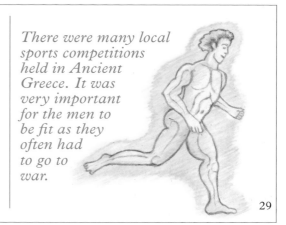

There were many local sports competitions held in Ancient Greece. It was very important for the men to be fit as they often had to go to war.

29

COMPREHENSION

1 Why was athletics important in Ancient Greece?

2 How many major competitions made up the Panhellenic Games?

3 When were the Olympic Games first officially recorded?

4 What types of building were erected for the Games?

5 Which two events would need horses?

6 How many events do you think made up the pentathlon?

7 The prizes awarded to the winners do not seem very special to us today. Why do you think the athletes were eager to take part in the Games?

8 How do you think we know so much about the Olympic Games which happened well over 2000 years ago?

If you were going to write a factual account of the Olympic Games in Ancient Greece, you would need to plan your work in the following way.

Stage 1 – **Research**
You would need to find reference books and encyclopedias which would give you some information about the topic.

Stage 2 – **Making notes**
You would need to make notes from these books. Remember: notes do not have to be written in full sentences.

Let's look at the sort of notes you could make from the four books on pages 28 and 29.

Book 1 – Life in Ancient Greece
4 major competitions = Panhellenic Games
people came from all over Greek world
buildings = for competitors, important people,
religious ceremonies
Temple of Zeus at Olympia, statue about 13 metres
high = one of the Seven Wonders of the Ancient World

Book 2 – The Ancient Greeks
Olympic Games in honour of Zeus
official records kept from 776 BC
sports = running, wrestling, boxing, chariot racing,
horse racing, pentathlon
prizes = olive wreaths, palm branches, woollen ribbons,
if athlete did really well = statue in his honour

Book 3 – The History of the Olympics
Olympics = most important of the Panhellenic Games
held every 4 years at Olympia
Stadium = running, wrestling, boxing
Hippodrome = horse and chariot racing

Book 4 – Peoples of the Past
lots of local sports competitions
important for men to be fit as they had to go to war

<u>Stage 3</u> – **Ordering your notes**
The notes give you information about five different aspects of the
Olympic Games. The next stage is to group the information together
under headings, for example:

why athletics was important
men had to be fit
often had to go to war

Panhellenic Games
four major competitions
competitors came from all over
the Greek world

Olympic Games
most important of the Panhellenic Games
official records began 776 BC
held every four years at Olympia
lasted one day until 77th Olympiad and
then 5 days in honour of Zeus

buildings
for competitors
for important people who came to watch
for religious ceremonies
statue of Zeus – about 13 metres high – one of
the Seven Wonders of the Ancient World

competitions and prizes
running, wrestling, boxing – in the Stadium
chariot and horse racing – in the Hippodrome
pentathlon
prizes = olive wreaths, palm branches,
woollen ribbons, statue for best athlete

You now have the information in five groups. Decide the order in which you want to put the information. This will give you five paragraphs:

paragraph 1 – why athletics was important

paragraph 2 – the Panhellenic Games

paragraph 3 – the Olympic Games

paragraph 4 – buildings

paragraph 5 – competitions and prizes

▲ If you found some other books about the early Olympic Games, in which paragraph would you put additional information about:

the buildings

the Panhellenic Games

the winners

Zeus

the importance of athletics to the Ancient Greeks?

Stage 4 – **Writing a first draft**

▲ Using the notes, write a factual account of the Olympic Games. When you have finished you will have written **the first draft**. This is not the finished piece of work.

Stage 5 – **Proofreading and revising**

Check 1 Have you written in paragraphs?

Check 2 Have you put in all the important information?

Check 3 Are your spellings correct? Use a dictionary for any words you are not sure about or any words that look wrong. Use a spellcheck if you are working on screen.

Check 4 Is your punctuation correct? Have you put in all the full stops and capital letters?

Stage 6 – **Present the final draft**

▲ Give your work a title.

▲ Write it out neatly. You may have produced a splendid piece of work but if it is untidy or messy and nobody wants to struggle to read it, it will all be wasted.

Now you have **the final draft**.

1 Find out about the Seven Wonders of the Ancient World.
Write a factual account about them.

2 Look for the names of the six sports in the Olympic Games.
Write a factual account about them.

Remember the stages:
Stage 1 – research
Stage 2 – making notes
Stage 3 – ordering your notes
Stage 4 – writing a first draft
Stage 5 – proofreading and revising
Stage 6 – present the final draft

PERSONAL CHOICE

Choose one of the following assignments:

1 Imagine you have taken part in a chariot race at the Olympic
Games. Write about your experience in three paragraphs:
paragraph 1 – how you got ready for the race and how you felt
paragraph 2 – the race itself: what happened and how you
felt about it
paragraph 3 – when the race had finished

2 Imagine you have been to the Olympic Games in Ancient
Greece and have watched all the races. Write a letter to
a friend describing what you saw and how you felt about it.

**WORKING WITH
WORDS**

'Panhellenic' comes from two Greek words:
pan = all   *hellenic* = Greek

The Panhellenic Games were open to all Greeks.

Can you find these *pan* words in your dictionary?

a cure for all things   pan _ _ _ _

a disease over a whole country   pan _ _ _ _ _

a complete suit of armour   pan _ _ _ _

a temple dedicated to all gods   pan _ _ _ _ _

Being young . . . being old

We go through many stages in our lives and each stage seems to have its own special problems.

Problems at school

In this extract from *Boy* by Roald Dahl, the author remembers how he was punished at school.

At the age of seven, Roald and his friends played a trick on Mrs Pratchett who owned the local sweet shop. They put a dead mouse into a jar of gobstoppers, which gave her a nasty shock. She came to school and identified the culprits. The boys were summoned to the Headmaster's study where Mrs Pratchett was waiting.

Thwaites knocked on the door.

'Enter!'

We sidled in. The room smelled of leather and tobacco. Mr Coombes was standing in the middle of it, dominating everything, a giant of a man if ever there was one, and in his hands he held a long yellow cane which curved round the top like a walking stick.

'I don't want any lies,' he said. 'I know very well you did it and you were all in it together. Line up over there against the bookcase . . .'

'You,' Mr Coombes said, pointing the cane at Thwaites, 'come over here.'

Thwaites went forward very slowly.

'Bend over,' Mr Coombes said.

Thwaites bent over. Our eyes were riveted on him. We were hypnotized by it all. We knew, of course, that boys got the cane now and again, but we had never heard of anyone being made to watch . . .

My own turn came at last. My mind was swimming and my eyes had gone all blurry as I went forward to bend over. I can remember wishing my mother would suddenly come bursting into the room shouting, 'Stop! How dare you do that to my son!' But she didn't. All I heard was Mrs Pratchett's dreadful high-pitched voice behind me screeching, 'This one's the cheekiest of the bloomin' lot, 'Eadmaster! Make sure you let 'im 'ave it good and strong!'

Mr Coombes did just that. As the first stroke landed and the pistol-crack sounded, I was thrown forward so violently that if my fingers hadn't been touching the carpet, I think I would have fallen flat on my face. As it was, I was able to catch myself on the palms of my hands and keep my balance. At first I heard only the *crack* and felt absolutely nothing at all, but a fraction of a second later the burning sting that flooded across my buttocks was so terrific that all I could do was gasp. I gave a great gushing gasp that emptied my lungs of every breath of air that was in them.

It felt, I promise you, as though someone had laid a red-hot poker against my flesh and was pressing down on it hard.

The second stroke was worse than the first and this was probably because Mr Coombes was well practised and had a splendid aim. He was able, so it seemed, to land the second one almost exactly across the narrow line where the first one had struck. It is bad enough when the cane lands on fresh skin, but when it comes down on bruised and wounded flesh, the agony is unbelievable.

The third one seemed even worse than the second . . .

By the time the fourth stroke was delivered, my entire backside seemed to be going up in flames.

Far away in the distance, I heard Mr Coombes's voice saying, 'Now get out.'

COMPREHENSION

Read the passage and answer the questions.

1   Why were the eyes of the other boys 'riveted' on Thwaites as he stepped forward to be caned?

2   When it was Roald Dahl's turn his mind was 'swimming' and his eyes had gone 'all blurry'.
    What does this tell us about the way he was feeling?

3   How does he describe what the first stroke of the cane felt like?

4   Why does Mr Coombes's voice sound 'far away in the distance' when he tells Roald Dahl to leave?

5   Do you think the punishment was fair or unfair?
    Give your reasons. How would you have punished the boys?

6   Have you ever played a joke on someone who did not see the funny side? Write about what happened. Remember this will be written in the **first person** – **I**.

Problems at home

Toby slammed the door shut. He would have stamped his foot
if there had been anywhere to stamp it. But that was part of the
problem. His bedroom floor was knee-deep in clutter. Simply to
get to the bed, he practically had to *wade* through games, models,
books, and hundreds of other bits and pieces.

And he'd been told to clear the whole lot up.

"No more excuses!" said Mum. "I don't even want to see your
face again, unless you're carrying some of that stuff out of your
room . . ."

He picked his way across the room to the safety of his bed. It
took real skill to know where to put down a foot and not squash
something, or snap something else. This wasn't simple mess, like
Sophie Hunter's bedroom. Her room was a pit. Disgusting! Crisp
packets, toffee wrappers, dirty socks – and *worse*. Toby didn't even
want to think about Sophie Hunter's bedroom.

No, Toby's was different. Everything jammed in his cupboards or
on his shelves, or spread out on his floor, was something he'd
wanted. Something he'd found or bought or swapped. Something
he'd brought home proudly and been glad to have. There was no
rubbish in here. And that was why he'd been sent to clear it out by
himself. Mum had offered several times before.

"I'll do it for you happily," she'd said. "But I must be allowed to
throw some things out."

Throw some things out? No way! Toby needed absolutely
everything. Well, maybe *needed* wasn't the right word.

Wanted.

He'd wanted everything. Rolling onto his stomach across the
duvet, he took a long hard look around the room. Catching sight of
one or two things, it was difficult to remember why he'd wanted
them so much. That Rubik cube, for example. Nobody played with
them any more. But any craze can come back. You never know . . .

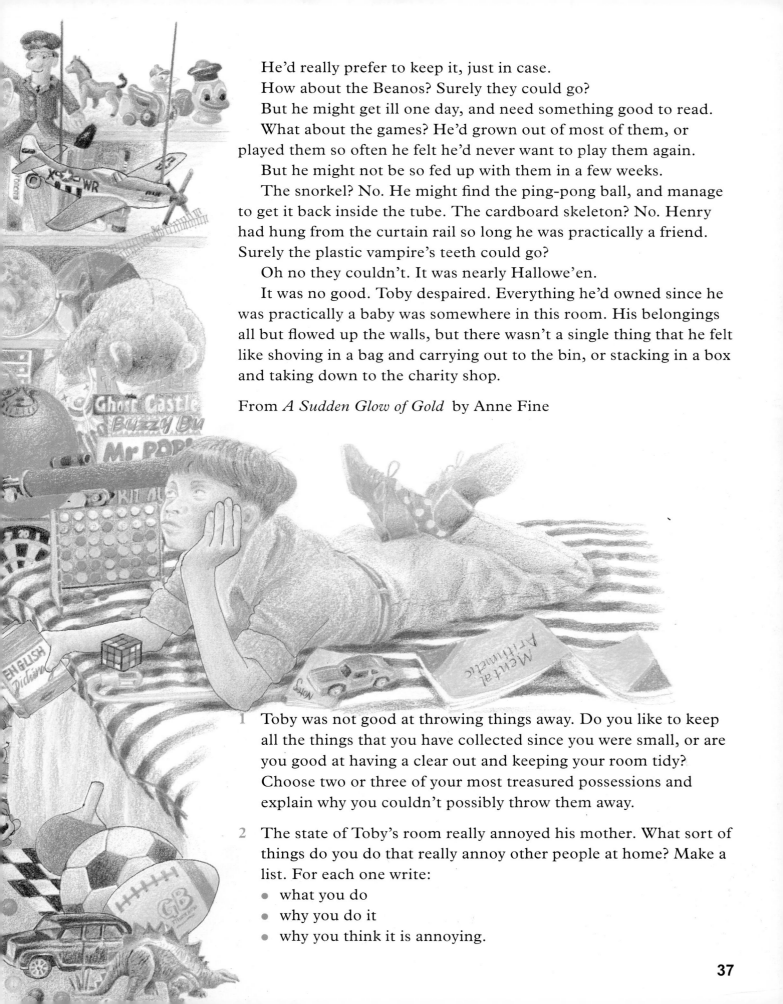

He'd really prefer to keep it, just in case.

How about the Beanos? Surely they could go?

But he might get ill one day, and need something good to read.

What about the games? He'd grown out of most of them, or played them so often he felt he'd never want to play them again.

But he might not be so fed up with them in a few weeks.

The snorkel? No. He might find the ping-pong ball, and manage to get it back inside the tube. The cardboard skeleton? No. Henry had hung from the curtain rail so long he was practically a friend. Surely the plastic vampire's teeth could go?

Oh no they couldn't. It was nearly Hallowe'en.

It was no good. Toby despaired. Everything he'd owned since he was practically a baby was somewhere in this room. His belongings all but flowed up the walls, but there wasn't a single thing that he felt like shoving in a bag and carrying out to the bin, or stacking in a box and taking down to the charity shop.

From *A Sudden Glow of Gold* by Anne Fine

1 Toby was not good at throwing things away. Do you like to keep all the things that you have collected since you were small, or are you good at having a clear out and keeping your room tidy? Choose two or three of your most treasured possessions and explain why you couldn't possibly throw them away.

2 The state of Toby's room really annoyed his mother. What sort of things do you do that really annoy other people at home? Make a list. For each one write:
- what you do
- why you do it
- why you think it is annoying.

Growing old

As we have seen, being young has its problems.
Growing old has its problems too!

Old Friends,
Old Friends.
Sat on their park bench
Like bookends.
A newspaper blown through the grass
Falls on the round toes
Of the high shoes
Of the Old Friends.

Old Friends,
Winter companions,
The old men
Lost in their overcoats,
Waiting for the sun.
The sounds of the city
Sifting through trees,
Settle like dust
On the shoulders
Of the Old Friends.

Can you imagine us
Years from today,
Sharing a park bench quietly?
How terribly strange
To be seventy.

From Old Friends by Paul Simon
© *Pattern Music Limited/*
Paul Simon 1968

1 Make a list of all the disadvantages you can think of about
  being old.

2 Make a list of the advantages of being old.

3 When you are old and have retired from work, what will you
  do to fill your time? Write about a typical day you would
  like to spend as an old person.

PERSONAL CHOICE

Choose one or two of the following assignments:

1 Imagine you could change places with your teacher or one of your parents for the day. They would have to do what you told them. What would you order them to do? Think of several things and describe each one in a paragraph of its own.

2 Do you have your own room at home or do you share a room? Each has advantages and disadvantages. Copy the headings and write down as many ideas as you can think of.

A room of my own   **Sharing a room**
advantages   disadvantages   advantages   disadvantages

3 Think of an old person whom you know. Imagine you are going to interview this old person about his/her life. Write a list of questions that you would like to ask.

WORKING WITH WORDS

When Roald Dahl describes the **pain** he felt when he was caned he uses the word **agony** to make the reader understand just how much it hurt.

Use your thesaurus and make a list of the other words he could have used.

Now use your thesaurus to find other words for:

smooth   popular   pale   ill   dirty

The first men on the moon

The first crisis the lunar explorers faced came just short of moonfall. The Apollo 11 Lunar Module, code-named 'Eagle', was still 9.5 km (6 miles) up when the vital guidance computer began flashing an alarm – it was overloading. Any second it could give up the ghost under the mounting pressure and nothing the two astronauts could do would save the mission. Emergencies were nothing new to commander Neil Armstrong but he and his co-pilot Buzz Aldrin hadn't even practised for this one on the ground – no one believed it could happen. Sweeping feet first towards their target, they pressed ahead as controllers on Earth waited heart-in-mouth. Racing against the computer, Eagle slowed and then pitched upright to 'stand' on its rocket plume and give Armstrong his first view of the landing site. The wrong one! They had overshot by four miles into unfamiliar territory and were heading straight for a football field size crater filled with boulders 'the size of Volkswagens'.

With his fuel running out, and only a minute's flying time left, Armstrong coolly accelerated the hovering Eagle beyond the crater, touching 88 kph (55 mph). Controllers were puzzled and alarmed by the unplanned manoeuvres. Mission Director George Hage pleaded silently: 'Get it down, Neil. Get it down.'

The seconds ticked away.

'Forward, drifting right,' Aldrin said. And then, with less than 20 seconds left, came the magic word: 'Contact!'

Armstrong spoke first: 'Tranquility Base here, the Eagle has landed.' His words were heard by 600 million people – a fifth of humanity.

About six and a half hours later, Eagle's front door was opened and Armstrong backed out onto a small porch. He wore a £42,000 moonsuit, a sort of Thermos flask capable of stopping micro-meteoroids travelling 30 times faster than a rifle bullet. He carried a backpack which weighed 49 kg and had enough oxygen for four hours. Heading down the ladder, Armstrong unveiled a £200,000 TV camera so the world could witness his first step: 'That's one small step for a man, one giant leap for mankind.' It was 3.56 am, 21 July, 1969.

Adapted from 'Man in Space' by Leo Enright from *The Encyclopedia of Space Travel and Astronomy*

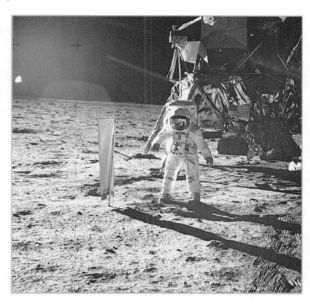

COMPREHENSION

Read the passage and answer the questions.

1 Why do you think the astronauts needed the 'guidance computer'? Where was it guiding them to?

2 What does the author mean when he writes 'They had **overshot** by four miles'?

3 What does the author mean when he writes 'Armstrong **coolly** accelerated the hovering Eagle'?

4 Why was 'Contact!' the magic word?

5 Why does the writer describe Armstrong's moonsuit as 'a sort of Thermos flask'? (Think about what a Thermos flask does.)

6 There were three astronauts on Apollo 11. Where do you think the third astronaut was when the Lunar Module landed on the moon?

7 The passage says 'with his fuel running out'. What does this mean? How do you think the astronauts leave the moon?

Can you imagine what the astronauts must have felt like when they made that trip and Neil Armstrong became the first human being to stand on the surface of the moon?

Let's look at the things that happened to the astronauts in the Lunar Module:

- the guidance computer was not working properly
- they were four miles from where they had planned to land
- they were heading for a crater with enormous boulders
- they had very little fuel left
- they only had 20 seconds to land
- they made a safe landing and were the first men to walk on the moon.

Both of them gave no sign of panic, but how do you think they were feeling inside?

▲ Imagine you were one of the astronauts on the Apollo 11 mission. Write an account of the moon landing and say how you were feeling:

- as you tried to land the Eagle
- as you stayed behind in the Command Module.

Earthrise from the moon

The 1960s were very exciting years in the 'space race'. Both America and the former USSR were spending a great deal of money to be the first to land on the moon. The chart below shows you the important events which took place before Neil Armstrong walked on the moon.

Date	Spacecraft	Occupants	Achievements
1957	Sputnik 2	USSR dog (Laika)	1st living creature in space
April 1961	Vostok 1	USSR Yuri Gagarin	1st human in space
May 1961	Mercury	USA Alan Shepard	1st American in space
Aug 1961	Vostok 2	USSR Gherman Titov	1st man to orbit the Earth
Feb 1962	Mercury	USA John Glenn	1st American to orbit the Earth
Aug 1962	Vostok 3	USSR Andrian Nikolayev	Passed within 3 miles (5 km)
	Vostok 4	USSR Pavel Popovich	of each other in space
June 1963	Vostok 6	USSR Valentina Tereshkova	1st woman in space
March 1965	Voskhod 2	USSR Alexei Leonov	1st man to walk in space
June 1965	Gemini 4	USA Edward White	1st American to walk in space
Dec 1968	Apollo 8	USA Frank Borman, Jim Lovell & Bill Anders	1st astronauts to orbit the moon
July 1969	Apollo 11	USA Buzz Aldrin Neil Armstrong	1st men on the moon

Look at the chart and answer the questions.

1 How many years were there between the first living creature going into space and the first men landing on the moon?

2 The chart lists three types of spacecraft used by the USSR. What are their names?

3 In the chart, what are the names of the spacecraft used by the USA? Can you suggest why these names were used?

4 Who was the first woman in space?

5 What 'first' did Alexei Leonov achieve?

6 Can you explain what the word 'orbit' means?

Russian dog 'Laika' – the first animal in space

43

For centuries humans have studied the heavens and dreamed of one day visiting far-off planets.

People have also thought that they could tell the future from the stars. This is called **astrology**. People born at different times of the year have different star signs or signs of the zodiac.

The twelve signs of the zodiac:

Birthday	Star sign	
21st March – 19th April	**Aries**	
20th April – 20th May	**Taurus**	
21st May – 21st June	**Gemini**	
22nd June – 22nd July	**Cancer**	
23rd July – 22nd August	**Leo**	
23rd August – 22nd September	**Virgo**	
23rd September – 23rd October	**Libra**	
24th October – 21st November	**Scorpio**	
22nd November – 21st December	**Saggitarius**	
22nd December – 19th January	**Capricorn**	
20th January – 18th February	**Aquarius**	
19th February – 20th March	**Pisces**	

1   When is your birthday?

2   What is your star sign?

3   Find out the star signs of the other people in your class. Make a graph to show the information.

4   Do you believe your future can be told through the stars?

PERSONAL CHOICE

Choose one or two of the following assignments:

1   Imagine you have walked on the surface of the moon. Write your diary entry for the day this happened. Remember to write about how you felt and describe what you saw.

2   When you read the passage by Leo Enright did you notice the cost of Armstrong's moonsuit and his camera? Sending spaceships into space costs millions of pounds. Do you think it is worth it? Could the money be better spent here on Earth? Make notes on **either** why you think it is worth the money **or** why you think it is not worth the money. Use your notes to write about your opinion.

3   Find the horoscope section in a daily newspaper. This is the part of the paper where an astrologer tells you what is going to happen to you that day. Find your star sign and read the horoscope. Now write a horoscope for one of your friends.

WORKING WITH WORDS

Find these expressions in the passage about the Apollo moon-landing and write what you think they mean in your own words.

'it could **give up the ghost**'
'controllers on Earth waited **heart-in-mouth**'.

Now do these.
What does it mean when we say:

1   She has a **heart of gold**.

2   He **took the bull by the horns**.

3   He is tied to his **mother's apron strings**.

4   She is **flogging a dead horse**.

5   He is **all fingers and thumbs**.

The aliens have landed!

The Earth has been ruled by the Tripods for many years. Inside the Tripods are the Masters who keep humans in their power by 'capping' them to control mind and body. Some people who have managed to escape capping have banded together to fight the Masters. Will Parker and two of his companions, all wearing false caps, have been taken into the Masters' city to be slaves. This is Will's first sight of the Masters!

For all the discomfort and fatigue, and fears as to what might happen, the first impulse I had was to laugh. They were so grotesque! They stood much taller than a man, nearly twice as tall, and were broad in proportion. Their bodies were wider at the bottom than the top, four or five feet around I thought, but tapered upwards to something like a foot in circumference at the head. If it *was* the head, for there was no break in the continuity, no sign of a neck. The next thing I noticed was that their bodies were supported not on two legs but three, these being thick but short. They had, matching them, three arms, or rather tentacles, issuing from a point about halfway up their bodies. And their eyes – I saw that there were three of those, too, set in a flattened triangle, one above and between the other two, a foot or so below the crown. In colour the creatures were green, though I saw that the shades differed, some being dark, the green tinged with brown, and others quite pallid. That, and the fact that their heights varied to some extent, appeared to be the only means of telling one from another. I felt it was a poor one.

Later I was to discover that, as one grew accustomed to them, identification was easier than I had expected. The orifices which were their mouths, and nose, and ears, varied too – in size, in shape a little, and in their relationship with each other. They were connected by a pattern of wrinkles and creases which one learned to know and recognize. At first impact, though, they were faceless, almost completely uniform. It sent a shiver of quite a different fear down my spine when one of them, stopping before me, spoke.

From *The City of Gold and Lead* by John Christopher

COMPREHENSION

1 Will experiences two sorts of fear. What is he frightened of?

2 Why do you think Will wanted to laugh when he first saw the Masters?

3 Make a list of the main differences between men and the Masters.

4 How did Will later come to be able to tell the Masters apart?

5 What do these words from the passage mean:

fatigue   circumference
pallid   orifices

The Day of the Triffids by John Wyndham

*John Wyndham's story tells of the planet Earth being taken over
by huge plants that can walk and sting people to death! At first,
people do not realise just what they have growing in their gardens.*

My introduction to a triffid came early.
It so happened that we had one of the first
in the locality growing in our garden . . .

Nobody, as far as I know, felt any
misgivings or alarm about them then.
I imagine that most people thought of them –
when they thought of them at all – in
much the same way that my father did.

I have a picture in my memory of him
examining ours and puzzling over it at
a time when it must have been about a year old . . .
My father leant over, peering at it through
his horn-rimmed glasses, fingering its stalk,
and blowing gently through his gingery moustache
as was his habit when thoughtful.
He inspected the straight stem, and the
woody bole from which it sprang.
He gave curious, if not very penetrative
attention to the three small, bare sticks
which grew up straight beside the stem.
He smoothed the short sprays of leathery green leaves
between his finger and thumb . . . Then he peered into
the curious funnel-like formation on top of the stem . . .

John Wyndham

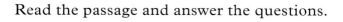 Read the passage and answer the questions.

1   How do you think people who had triffids growing in
their gardens felt about it at first?

2   At this point in the story how does the writer want you
to feel about the triffids?

3   Imagine you and another member of your family found
a triffid in your garden. Write your conversation.

Remember
your speech
marks.

48

WRITING YOUR OWN SCIENCE FICTION STORY

Writing about what might happen in the future is called science fiction. Sometimes science fiction becomes science fact! HG Wells wrote a book called *The First Men in the Moon* many years before men actually landed there. Luckily for us *The War of the Worlds* and *The Day of the Triffids* are still science fiction!

Writing a science fiction story needs careful planning, like any story, and a great deal of imagination.

Some science fiction stories are set here on Earth. Others are set in different worlds that the characters are visiting. Decide if your characters:

- are involved with aliens who have invaded the Earth. Choose a familiar place so that you can describe it clearly.

- have travelled to another planet. You can let your imagination take over and describe a really weird and wonderful place.

Setting

Characters

The kind of characters you have will depend on the setting you have chosen.

- If your story takes place on Earth then the characters can be ordinary people. The aliens have to be able to breathe and move around in our atmosphere or have machines that enable them to do this. Are the aliens friendly or unfriendly? Do the humans want to be friends or are they too scared?

- If your story takes place on another planet then your characters are likely to be astronauts and scientists and *they* will be the aliens! The creatures that live on the planet will be able to breathe and move more easily than the humans. Are the creatures friendly or unfriendly? Why have the humans come to this planet?

Plot

You must think very carefully about what is going to happen and this will depend on your characters and setting. Think about what would happen if:

- aliens came to Earth and were unfriendly
- aliens came to Earth and were friendly
- the astronauts met unfriendly creatures on the planet they visited
- the astronauts met friendly creatures on the planet they visited.

Whatever you do, don't just have them meeting and fighting. That would be very boring!

▲ Now write your own science fiction story.

PERSONAL CHOICE

Choose one or two of these assignments:

1 Imagine you are a newspaper reporter and you are writing a report about the first sighting of a triffid. Remember:
   - an interesting headline
   - illustrations
   - facts/opinions/interviews/eye-witness accounts.

2 Is there life on other planets?
   Make notes of all the reasons why you think there is life on other planets and notes of all the reasons why you think there is no life on other planets. Use your notes to write two paragraphs:
   paragraph 1: reasons why you think there is life on other planets
   paragraph 2: reasons why you think there is no life on other planets

3 HG Wells was one of the first science fiction writers. Find out what you can about him and present your work in a written report. Look at page 33 to remind you of the stages in this type of writing.

WORKING WITH WORDS

Both John Christopher and John Wyndham describe the aliens that have come to Earth in great detail. They 'paint a picture with words' so that the reader has a very clear idea of what the characters in the story see. Look at this space creature.

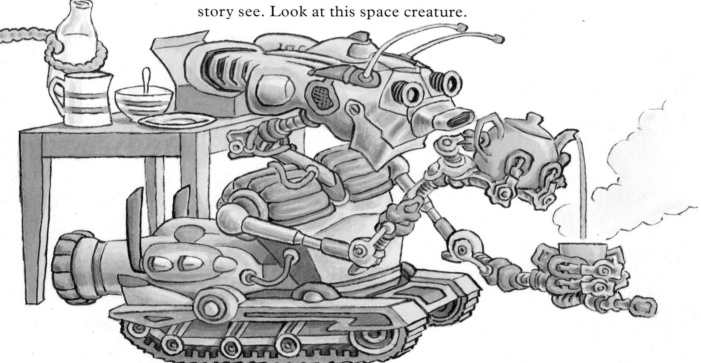

▲ Write a clear description of the space creature.
Use your thesaurus to help you find interesting words.

Children in wartime

Anne Frank and her parents were German Jews who emigrated to Holland in 1933. On 9th July, 1942 they went into hiding to avoid being rounded up by the Nazis and sent to a concentration camp. Her parents, her sister Margot and herself, together with another family, the Van Daans, lived in the two upper floors of an old building for over two years. During that time Anne kept a diary. Here are some extracts.

Anne Frank's house

Interior of Anne Frank's house

Thursday, 9th July, 1942

I will describe the building . . . There is a small landing at the top . . .

The right door leads to our 'Secret Annexe'. No one would ever guess that there would be so many rooms hidden behind that plain, grey door. There's a little step in front of the door and then you are inside.

There is a steep staircase immediately opposite the entrance. On the left a tiny passage brings you into a room which was to become the Frank family's bed-sitting-room, next door a smaller room, study and bedroom for the two young ladies of the family. On the right a little room without windows containing the washbasin and a small W.C. compartment, with another door leading to Margot's and my room. If you go up the next flight of stairs and open the door, you are simply amazed that there could be such a big light room in such an old house by the canal. There is a gas stove in this room . . . and a sink. This is now the kitchen for the Van Daan couple, besides being general living-room, dining-room, and scullery.

A tiny little corridor room will become Peter Van Daan's apartment. Then . . . there is a large attic. So there you are, I've introduced you to the whole of our beautiful 'Secret Annexe'.

Extract from diary

Anne Frank

Wednesday, 13th January, 1943

Everything has upset me again this morning . . .

It is terrible outside. Day and night more of those poor miserable people are being dragged off, with nothing but a rucksack and a little money. On the way they are deprived even of these possessions. Families are torn apart, the men, women and children are all being separated. Children coming home from school find that their parents have disappeared. Women return from shopping to find their homes shut up and their families gone.

The Dutch people are anxious too, their sons are being sent to Germany. Everyone is afraid.

Monday, 26th July, 1943

It was about two o'clock . . . when the sirens began to wail . . . we had not been upstairs five minutes when they began shooting hard, so much so that we went and stood in the passage. And yes, the house rumbled and shook, and down came the bombs.

I clasped my 'escape bag' close to me, more because I wanted to have something to hold than with an idea of escaping, because there's nowhere we can go. If ever we come to the extremity of fleeing from here, the street would be just as dangerous as an air raid. This one subsided after half an hour . . .

That evening at dinner: another air-raid alarm! It was a nice meal, but at the sound of the alert my hunger vanished . . . 'Oh, dear me, twice in one day, that's too much,' we all thought, but that didn't help at all; once again the bombs rained down . . .

From *The Diary of Anne Frank*

COMPREHENSION

Read the diary extracts and answer the questions.

1   When Anne is writing on 9th July, 1942, it is her first day in hiding. What kind of mood is she in? What words could you use to describe her feelings?

2   In the extract on 13th January, 1943, Anne has been in hiding for six months. How is she feeling now? What sort of things is she writing about?

3   In the extract of 26th July, 1943, Anne has now not been outside for a whole year. Look carefully at what she has written and describe how she is feeling.

WRITING A DIARY

We have looked at writing a diary in earlier books. You were asked to record things that happened to you and write a little about how you felt.

Anne Frank's diary is much more than that. She wrote a lot about what happened every day but she also wrote about the things that worried her, her relationship with her parents, her hopes for the future.

1   Write three diary extracts, based on your own experience.

▲ (9th July, 1942) Anne describes her surroundings in a lot of detail. Choose your own home or school and write a description and draw a plan. You need to remember:

- that your audience will probably not have seen what you are describing so you must be very exact.
- that the way you write – the words you choose – will tell your audience whether you like what you are describing or you dislike it.

▲ (13th January, 1943) Anne describes what is going on around her. Find out about one important news story that is happening now and write about it in your diary extract. Remember you can:

- look at newspapers and listen to the radio or television news
- talk to adults about what is going on
- write about something that is happening in this country or in another part of the world.

▲ (26th July, 1943) Anne describes what it is like to be in a frightening situation. Have you ever been frightened? Write about what happened and how you felt. You need to remember:

- that you might be writing about something that wouldn't frighten you now, but did at the time. Try to describe it clearly so that your audience can understand why you were frightened.

2   Try keeping your own diary.

- Write in a notebook and put the date at the beginning of each day's entry.
- You do not need to write every day. Write when something interesting happens or there is something you want to remember.

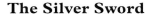

The Silver Sword

The story of Anne Frank is a true one, and the story of *The Silver Sword* is also based on events which really happened in Poland during the Second World War.

The parents of Bronia, Edek and Ruth are taken away by German soldiers and the three children are left to fend for themselves. They escape from their home and wander the streets trying to find somewhere else to live.

They made their new home in a cellar at the other end of the city. They had tunnelled their way into it. From the street it looked like a rabbit's burrow in a mound of rubble, with part of a wall rising behind. On the far side there was a hole in the lower part of the wall, and this let in light and air as well as rain.

When they asked the Polish Council of Protection about their mother, they were told she had been taken off to Germany to work on the land. Nobody could say which part of Germany. Though they went many times to ask, they never found out any more. 'The war will end soon,' they were told. 'Be patient, and your mother will come back.'

But the war dragged on, and their patience was to be sorely tried.

They quickly made their new home as comfortable as they could. Edek, who could climb like a monkey, scaled three storeys of a bombed building to fetch a mattress and some curtains. The mattress he gave to Ruth and Bronia. The curtains made good sheets. On wet days they could be used over the hole in the wall to keep the rain out. With floorboards he made two beds, chairs and a table. With bricks from the rubble he built a wall to divide the cellar into two rooms, one to live in and one to sleep in. He stole blankets from a Nazi supply dump, one for each of them.

Here they lived for the rest of that winter and the following spring.

Food was not easy to find. Ruth and Bronia had green Polish ration cards and were allowed to draw the small rations that the Nazis allowed. But, except when Edek found casual work, they had no money to buy food. Edek had no ration card. He had not dared to apply for one, as that would have meant disclosing his age. Everyone over twelve had to register, and he would almost certainly have been carried off to Germany as a slave worker.

Whenever possible they ate at the soup kitchens which Polish Welfare had set up. Sometimes they begged at a nearby convent. Sometimes they stole from the Nazis or scrounged from their garbage bins. They saw nothing wrong in stealing from their enemies, but they were careful never to steal from their own people.

From *The Silver Sword* by Ian Serraillier

COMPREHENSION Read the passage and answer the questions.

1 What does the author mean when he writes 'their patience was to be sorely tried'?

2 Who do you think the Nazis were?

3 In what ways did the three children manage to get food?

4 Living in the cellar on their own must have given the children many problems. Apart from the difficulty of finding food, what other problems do you think they had?

Evacuation

Many children who lived in the big cities in Britain were sent to the countryside during the war. Carrie and her brother Nicholas were sent from London to Wales.

Sheep and mountains. 'Oh, it'll be such fun,' their mother had said when she kissed them goodbye at the station. 'Living in the country instead of the stuffy old city. You'll love it, you see if you don't!' As if Hitler had arranged this old war for their benefit, just so that Carrie and Nick could be sent away in a train with gas masks slung over their shoulders and their names on cards round their necks. Labelled like parcels – Caroline Wendy Willow and Nicholas Peter Willow – only with no address to be sent to. None of them, not even the teachers, knew where they were going. 'That's part of the adventure,' Carrie's mother had said, and not just to cheer them up: it was her nature to look on the bright side. If she found herself in Hell, Carrie thought now, she'd just say, 'Well, at least we'll be *warm*.'

Thinking of her mother, always making the best of things (or pretending to; when the train began to move she had stopped smiling) Carrie nearly did cry. There was a lump like a pill stuck in her throat. She swallowed hard and pulled faces.

From *Carrie's War* by Nina Bawden

Ruth and Carrie were about the same age when they had to face life without their parents.

Read the passages again carefully.

1   Imagine you are Ruth and write a diary entry at the end of the day when your parents were taken away and you found a new home in the cellar.

2   Imagine you are Carrie and write a diary entry at the end of the day when you have left your mother at the station and gone to live with strangers in Wales.

PERSONAL CHOICE   Choose one of the following assignments:

1   Imagine you are Carrie's mother and write a letter to a friend after you have put your children on the train to go to Wales. Explain how you felt and how you think the children felt.

2   Some people refuse to fight if their country goes to war. They are called conscientious objectors. Do you agree with them? Make some notes on why some people think it is wrong to fight and some notes on why other people think there are times when you should.

WORKING WITH WORDS

Carrie's mother always looked on the bright side of things. This is called being **optimistic**.

Choose the right word from the box to explain these:

1   expecting the worst to happen

2   lifelike

3   thinking there is nothing you can do that will make any difference

fatalistic   realistic   pessimistic

The Loch Ness monster

For the past 1400 years there have been sightings of the famous monster in the murky waters of Loch Ness in Scotland. The loch is 270 metres deep in some places and is said to be the home of a prehistoric monster affectionately known as 'Nessie'.

The earliest story about the monster goes back to AD 565 when the Irish saint, Columba, is said to have seen the monster. The story says that a disciple of Columba was swimming across the loch when the monster appeared suddenly 'with a great roar and open mouth'. Saint Columba made the sign of the cross, asked for God's protection and said to the monster, 'Think not to go further, nor touch not that man. Quick, go back . . . ' The monster apparently obeyed and has never been known to hurt anyone.

Over the next fourteen centuries there have been many recorded sightings of Nessie but it wasn't until 1934 that the monster was allegedly captured in a photograph. A London surgeon, holidaying in Scotland, was driving by the loch and took a photograph of what he claimed was the monster.

It showed a long neck and a thick body and was published in the London Daily Mail.

People's opinions were divided. Those who really believed that the monster existed said that the photograph fitted the description given by others who claimed to have seen it. Those who did not believe in the monster said that the photograph showed rotting vegetation floating on the surface or perhaps the tail of a diving otter.

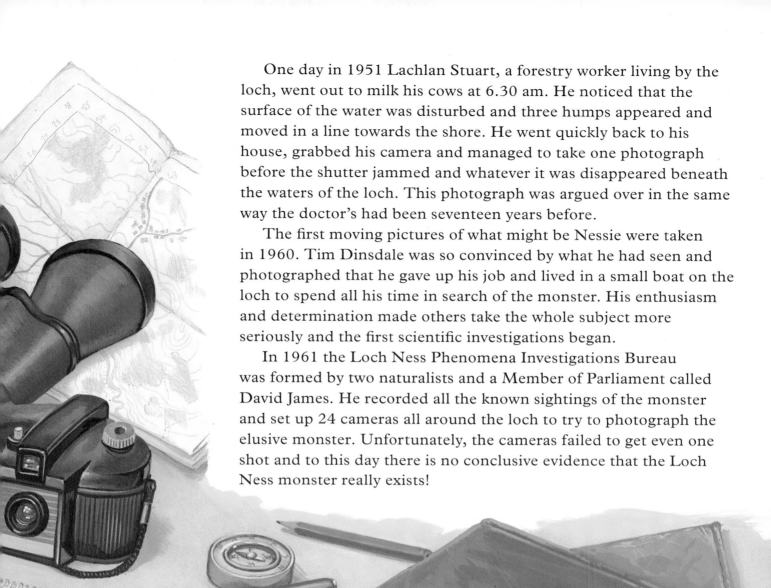

One day in 1951 Lachlan Stuart, a forestry worker living by the loch, went out to milk his cows at 6.30 am. He noticed that the surface of the water was disturbed and three humps appeared and moved in a line towards the shore. He went quickly back to his house, grabbed his camera and managed to take one photograph before the shutter jammed and whatever it was disappeared beneath the waters of the loch. This photograph was argued over in the same way the doctor's had been seventeen years before.

The first moving pictures of what might be Nessie were taken in 1960. Tim Dinsdale was so convinced by what he had seen and photographed that he gave up his job and lived in a small boat on the loch to spend all his time in search of the monster. His enthusiasm and determination made others take the whole subject more seriously and the first scientific investigations began.

In 1961 the Loch Ness Phenomena Investigations Bureau was formed by two naturalists and a Member of Parliament called David James. He recorded all the known sightings of the monster and set up 24 cameras all around the loch to try to photograph the elusive monster. Unfortunately, the cameras failed to get even one shot and to this day there is no conclusive evidence that the Loch Ness monster really exists!

COMPREHENSION

Use your dictionary to help you.

Read the passage and answer the questions.

1 How deep is Loch Ness?

2 When was the monster first photographed?

3 What did people think of the photograph?

4 Who published the photograph?

5 Who gave up his job to search for the monster?

6 Do you think that Nessie exists? Give reasons for your answer.

7 Explain the meaning of:

    murky waters   prehistoric   naturalist

           phenomena   elusive monster

WRITING IN PARAGRAPHS

The passage about the Loch Ness monster is a factual piece of writing.

Can you remember the stages for this type of work?

Stage 1 – research

Stage 2 – making notes

Stage 3 – ordering your notes

Stage 4 – writing a first draft

Stage 5 – proofreading/revising

Stage 6 – present the final draft

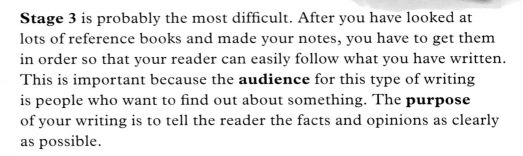

Stage 3 is probably the most difficult. After you have looked at lots of reference books and made your notes, you have to get them in order so that your reader can easily follow what you have written. This is important because the **audience** for this type of writing is people who want to find out about something. The **purpose** of your writing is to tell the reader the facts and opinions as clearly as possible.

The way to do this is to think of each paragraph in turn and decide what it is going to be about.

Look again at the passage about the Loch Ness monster. There are eight paragraphs and each one tells you something different about the search for Nessie.

▲ Make a chart like the one below and say what each paragraph is about. The first two are done for you.

Paragraph	What it is about
1	Introduces the Loch Ness monster so the reader knows what the passage is going to be about.
2	St Columba and his disciple seeing the monster

PHOTOGRAPHIC EVIDENCE

This is the picture taken by Lachlan Stuart in 1951.

▲ Imagine you are a naturalist who has been asked to study the photograph and report what you think. You have not yet come to an opinion as to whether or not the monster exists. Write your report in paragraphs:

paragraph 1 – describe what you see in the picture

paragraph 2 – give all the reasons you can for it being the Loch Ness monster

paragraph 3 – give all the reasons you can for it **not** being the Loch Ness monster

paragraph 4 – write what your opinion is after studying the photograph

EYE-WITNESS ACCOUNT

This is an eye-witness account by the Warden at the Youth Hostel at Altsaigh on the shores of Loch Ness. One day in 1949 he was working at the back of the hostel.

'On looking up,' said the warden, 'I noticed a strange-looking object about 800 yards away. The water was absolutely calm and the object was pretty well in line between myself and Foyers (on the opposite side of the loch).

'After a minute or two the object changed in shape and what I took to be the head and neck were raised above the water and a large hump could be seen behind. I was just thinking of calling my wife and the assistant warden when the Monster sank, leaving quite a surge on the surface of the loch. After a moment or two, to my surprise, it came up again. I then called my assistant Colin Cameron, who arrived in time to see three humps, each about ten feet long, while about ten feet separated each hump. The creature travelled along in this form, its speed being at least 30 miles an hour and, believe me, it must be an enormous creature having regard to the size of the humps which stood two or three feet above the water.

'I then fetched binoculars from the house and had another excellent view. The skin, I thought, resembled that of an elephant. The Monster dived again, this time in the direction of Fort Augustus and did not reappear.'

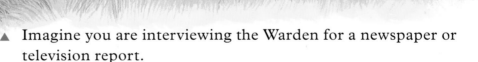

▲ Imagine you are interviewing the Warden for a newspaper or television report.

Use the facts in the passage to write questions and answers. You can begin like this:

Interviewer: What were you doing when you first saw the monster?

Warden: I was working at the back of the Youth Hostel. I looked up and saw a strange-looking object about 800 yards away.

Interviewer: Are you sure you had a clear view?

Warden: The water was very calm and the object was pretty well in line between myself and Foyers so I did have a good view.

Continue the interview, setting it out in the same way.

PERSONAL CHOICE

Choose one of the following assignments:

1 Imagine you are the Loch Ness monster. Write a description of what it is like to live in the murky deep water of the loch. You will obviously describe what you see both down below and when you surface, but don't forget about the other senses – what you feel, smell, hear and touch.

2 There are many legends about strange animals known as werewolves. Find out what you can about them and use your notes to write a report. Remember you should be looking for the facts that are known about them and any opinions you can find.

WORKING WITH WORDS

A **naturalist** studies animals and plants. What do these people study?

biologist   geologist   zoologist   botanist   chemist

Owen Glendower

In the fifteenth century Henry IV ruled England and Wales. The Welsh wanted to rule themselves and Owen Glendower led the people in revolt against the English king. There are many stories about his daring deeds. This is one about his escape from capture.

Owen Glendower was a prince of the royal Welsh blood in the time of King Henry IV. In his own country he was called Owain Glyndwr, but the English lords at the court of King Henry, where Owen was a courtier and soldier, found it easier to say 'Glendower'. These noblemen used to sneer at Owen and call him 'barefoot Welshman' and when one of them, Lord Grey of Ruthin, stole some of Owen's lands the young prince decided that the time had come to fight against his enemies. He went back to Wales, proclaimed himself Prince of Wales by right, and called on all Welsh fighting men to help him free their country from English rule.

For a time the rebellion succeeded. Owen's men won fight after fight against the men-at-arms which the English lords sent to conquer them. But when King Henry ordered a large army to march into Wales and capture the Prince, the tide of battle turned and the Welsh were defeated. Owen's fighting-men began to desert him and soon he was left quite alone in the mountains of North Wales, with King Henry's soldiers hunting for him in every valley.

The Prince had a good friend who lived near Beddgelert, close to the highest mountain in Wales. This was Rhys Goch Eryri – Red Reece of Snowdon – and he was called 'Red' because of his fiery-red hair and beard. Journeying by night, Owen came to Reece's house and knocked cautiously on the door. When his friend saw who it was he welcomed the Prince warmly and told him he should stay as long as he wished.

"Danger brings me here, Reece," said Owen, "and I bring danger with me, for if I am found in your house the King's men will hang you."

"I'll chance that," laughed Red Reece. "One of my fellows shall keep watch up the Colwyn valley, for that's the way Henry's soldiers will come, if they come at all."

So Owen found refuge there, and for a short time his hiding-place was not discovered. Then, one morning, Reece's watchman came racing up to the house to report a large force of the King's men approaching along the Colwyn valley.

"You have been betrayed, my lord Prince," said Reece.

"They will surely come to search my house. You and I must take to the mountains and hide."

Owen shook his head. "I am the hunted one, not you," he said. "I go alone."

"I go with you," Red Reece told him firmly. "Quick – put on this old cloak and hat, and I'll dress myself in the same way. If they see us they'll think we're a couple of servants."

Owen did as he said, and they slipped out of the back door onto the hillside just as the soldiers approached the front door and spread out to surround the house. Some leafy thickets gave good cover for Owen and Reece at first and they scrambled up the lower hillside without being seen. But on the bare rocky slope above there was no cover, and a keen-eyed soldier down by the house saw them and reported that two servants were running away from the house.

"Running away?" said the captain of the troop. "Then one of them will be Glendower. After them, men!"

Up the hillside rushed the soldiers like a pack of hounds on the scent. Luckily for the fugitives there were no bowmen among them, or they would have been shot down. But the soldiers, armed with swords and daggers, were men picked specially for this sort of chase and they were as fast over steep rough ground as Owen and Reece.

"They'll have us yet," panted Reece as they ran. "You dodge aside when we get behind the rocks yonder – I'll lead them straight on."

The pursuers were hot on their heels and there was no time to argue. Owen ducked out of sight and Reece, with a defiant yell, raced on. The soldiers followed him. And then Reece's hat flew from his head, revealing his fiery-red hair and beard.

"That red fox isn't Glendower!" shouted the captain. "Look – there goes our man!"

Owen was running downhill towards the Pass of Aberglaslyn. In those days the sea came right up to the western end of the Pass, and his plan was to reach it and escape by boat. But the captain of the troop guessed what he was about and sent his fastest runners to cut him off. Owen was forced to swerve back to the right, in the direction of the big mountain called Moel Hebog which stands above Beddgelert. He splashed across the River Glaslyn, thigh-deep in the water, and climbed as fast as he could up the rough hillside. Behind him the pursuing soldiers spread out in a wide crescent to prevent him from escaping to one side or the other. Soon he was high up on Moel Hebog, with the dark cliffs that defend its summit close above him.

Owen had hoped to cross the ridge on the left and escape into Cwm Pennant on the other side. But now he saw the soldiers closing in on that side and knew he could never reach the ridge. He made across to the right – but there too were the clambering figures of King Henry's men. He was being driven up against the foot of the cliffs, and no man had ever found a way to climb them. Owen Glendower was trapped. If you look up at Moel Hebog from Beddgelert you'll see the cliffs stretching away to the left below the top of the mountain. You may be able to make out the dark line of a cleft in the middle of the cliffs. Owen Glendower saw this cleft just when it seemed certain that he would be captured, and climbed up towards it at top speed. It was as steep and narrow as a chimney and nearly three hundred feet from bottom to top, but it was his only chance and he got into it and began to climb. One slip and he really would have fallen into the hands of his enemies, probably with a broken neck. But Owen was a fine cragsman and he didn't slip. By the time the breathless soldiers reached the foot of the cleft he was more than halfway to the top. The captain ordered his troop to follow, but every man refused. They were soldiers, they said, not mountain-goats! The captain decided that he wasn't a mountain-goat either, and they gave up the chase and retreated down the mountainside. As for Owen Glendower, he climbed out at the top of the chimney and made his way to a cave in the side of a mountain called Moel yr Ogof (you can see it from the road a mile north of Beddgelert) where he hid himself in safety. Red Reece kept him secretly supplied with food until the soldiers had left the valley, and then Owen came out of hiding to rally his men and fight once more against his enemies.

From *Welsh Tales for Children* by Showell Styles

1 The English nobles called Glendower 'barefoot Welshman'. What does this tell you about their attitude towards him?

2 Why do you think Owen knocked 'cautiously' on Reece's door?

3 How did the captain know that one of the servants was Owen?

4 What does 'the pursuers were hot on their heels' mean?

5 Why did the soldiers refuse to chase Owen up the cleft?

WRITING ADVENTURE STORIES

Adventure stories – like any stories – need careful planning.
Read the story of Owen Glendower again and answer the questions.

1 Setting

Very often an author will use different settings in a story as
characters move from place to place. In the story of Owen
Glendower you should be able to find seven different settings.
Make a list of them in the order in which they occur in the story.

2 Characters

There are two main characters in the story. Write their names.
Make some notes on what we find out about each of them.
Remember, we find out about characters by:

- what the author tells us
- what the character says and does

3 Plot

What actually happens in the story?
You should be able to write the plot in about ten lines.
Do not include what any of the characters says.
Concentrate on what happens.

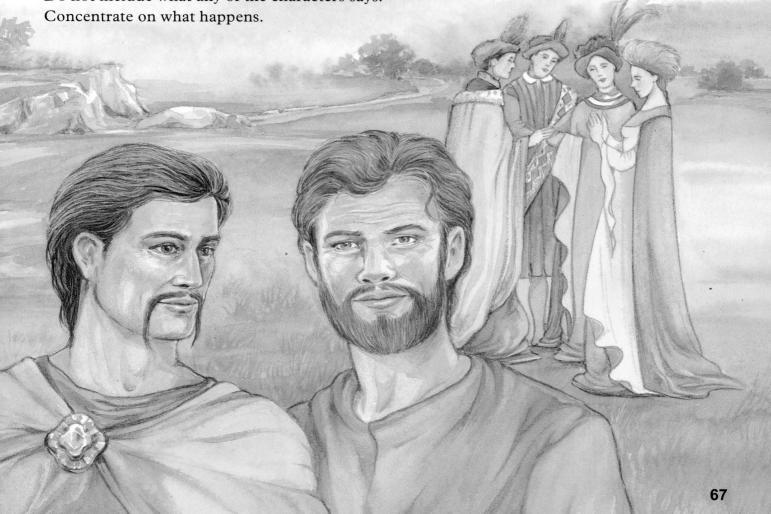

People who read adventure stories expect the story to be exciting and have them 'on the edge of their seat'. The main character is usually in some sort of danger or has to do something daring or frightening.

Owen Glendower's escape story is like this. We do not know until the very end whether Owen will escape and at one point in the story we are convinced he is going to be caught.

If we look at the plot of the story we can see how the author has planned to keep the reader guessing:

- Owen decides he is going to fight the English.

- He gathers an army together and is very successful – everything goes right for him.

- Henry sends a bigger army and Owen is defeated – everything goes wrong for him.

- He goes to Red Reece – things are going well again as Red Reece will hide him.

- King Henry's men find out where he is hiding – things look bad again.

- Owen and Red escape dressed as servants – things look better and the reader thinks Owen might escape.

- Owen is trapped on all sides by the soldiers – things are looking very bad indeed and the reader thinks there is no escape for him.

- Owen sees the cleft in the cliffs and makes a daring climb to safety – a happy ending to the story.

▲ Write your own adventure story in the same way. Work out the plot so that things go first well, then badly for the main character. Keep the reader guessing as to how your story will end.

Choose one of the following assignments:

1 The place Beddgelert is mentioned in the story
and there is a legend connected with it. It is
about Prince Llewelyn and his dog
Gelert. Find out what you can about
what happened and retell the story
in your own words.

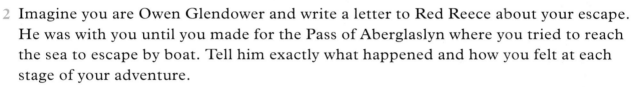

2 Imagine you are Owen Glendower and write a letter to Red Reece about your escape.
He was with you until you made for the Pass of Aberglaslyn where you tried to reach
the sea to escape by boat. Tell him exactly what happened and how you felt at each
stage of your adventure.
Remember to set out your letter correctly.

WORKING WITH WORDS

Owen was trapped by the soldiers at the bottom of the cliffs
which no one had ever been able to climb. He did not have
a choice if he was to escape. In this situation we could say:

Necessity is the mother of invention

This is a **proverb** which means that something which is considered
impossible, suddenly becomes possible when there is no choice.

Explain the meaning of these proverbs:

1 Once bitten, twice shy.

2 It never rains but it pours.

3 Killing two birds with one stone.

4 You can't make a silk purse out of a sow's ear.

5 Using a steam hammer to crack a nut.

Tutankhamun's Gold

EGYPT

Valley of the Kings • Luxor

River Nile

Howard Carter was growing desperate. For nearly 20 years he had searched for the tomb of the boy king, Tutankhamun. Now money to finance his quest was running out . . .

What made the prospect of failure harder to bear was that the English scholar remained convinced that the tomb was somewhere in the Valley of the Kings, site of the ancient capital of Thebes, for there were inscriptions about Tutankhamun in the nearby temple of Luxor. He believed too that the tomb had never been looted, for no relics had ever been reported.

But all he had found – 15 years before – were jars of clothes bearing the king's name. Since then Carter had explored nearly the whole floor of the valley and found no trace of the pharaoh, who had died at the age of 18.

As Carter trudged through the dawn-cool sand to his diggings, he thought again of his patron, the amateur archaeologist Lord Carnarvon, and remembered their last meeting in England. Carnarvon had wanted to call off the search. 'It has cost me a fortune,' he told Carter. 'I can't afford it.'

But Carter pleaded with him to finance one last try. 'All right, Howard,' Carnarvon laughed. 'I'm a gambler. I'll back you for one more toss. If it is a loss then I am through. Where do we begin?' Carter showed him a map of the valley, indicating a small triangular area not yet explored as it was on the approach to the tomb of Ramses VI. 'There,' he told his patron. 'It's the last place left.'

Now, as he approached his diggings,

Carter wrote later about his first sight of the inside of the tomb:
'At first I could see nothing, the hot air from the chamber causing the candle flames to flicker. But as my eyes grew accustomed to the light, details of the room emerged slowly from the mist: strange animals, statues and gold – everywhere the glint of gold. For the moment – an eternity it must have seemed to others standing by – I was struck dumb with amazement; and when Lord Carnarvon, unable to stand the suspense any longer, inquired anxiously, "Can you see anything?" it was all I could do to get out the words: "Yes – wonderful things." '

Howard Carter and his assistant

Mask of Tutankhamun

Carter reflected that this looked like a dismal end to his dream. He and his workmen had found nothing but the rubble of huts that had been used by the labourers building the tomb of Ramses. For three days they had hacked at the rubble and found nothing.

When Carter reached the site his foreman, Ali, ran over. 'We have uncovered a step cut into the ground,' he said. Within two days they had cleared a steep staircase that led down to a sealed door. Carter immediately sent a telegram to Carnarvon:

AT LAST HAVE MADE WONDERFUL DISCOVERY IN VALLEY STOP A MAGNIFICENT TOMB WITH SEALS INTACT STOP RE-COVERED SAME FOR YOUR ARRIVAL CONGRATULATIONS

The date was November 6th, 1922.

Egypt was a powerful country for 3000 years. During that time it had 300 rulers known as pharaohs. Tutankhamun reigned in Egypt in the 14th century BC. He was only a boy when he came to the throne and died ten years later. Although we know little about him he is probably the most famous of the pharaohs thanks to Carter's discovery of his tomb.

The pyramids at Giza

Read all the information about Tutankhamun and answer the questions.

1 Who was paying for Howard Carter to search for the tomb of Tutankhamun?

2 What two reasons made Howard Carter convinced that the tomb was in the Valley of the Kings?

3 Where was the part of the Valley of the Kings that Carter had not yet explored?

4 What news did the foreman, Ali, have for Carter?

5 Why was it so important to Carter that the seals of the tomb were 'intact'?

6 Write in your own words what Carter felt when he first looked into the tomb.

Tomb of Tutankhamun

WRITING A MAGAZINE ARTICLE

The information about Tutankhamun is set out in the style of a magazine article.

Some magazines are about one particular subject like fishing, cookery or do-it-yourself. Other magazines are more general and have articles about many different sorts of things. No matter what sort of magazine it is, the articles are there for two main reasons:

● to inform the reader

● to interest the reader

The reader – *how will the reader be informed?*

The main point of the article is to inform the reader how Howard Carter discovered the tomb of Tutankhamun.

What other information does the article give to help the reader understand? Look at:

the boxes   the map   the pictures

▲ Make some notes on how you think these help to inform the reader.

The reader – *how will the reader's interest be captured?*

Look again at the two pages about Tutankhamun.

How has the writer made the pages look interesting? Look at:

- the way the text is set out
- the use of colour
- the use of pictures and maps

▲ Make some notes on how you think these help to interest the reader.

The writer – *how to inform the reader*

As with all factual writing the writer has to find out about the subject.

Remember the stages:
- research
- making notes
- ordering your notes
- writing a first draft
- proofreading/revising
- present the final draft

The writer – *how to interest the reader*

Capturing the interest of the reader has a lot to do with how the article **looks** on the page. You have to make the reader interested before they start reading. A complete page of text doesn't look very interesting. You can make it look more inviting to the reader by:

- using illustrations – maps, photographs, drawings etc
- breaking the text up by using boxes, different coloured background etc

▲ Look through some magazines and see how articles look on the page.

▲ Choose one that **looks** interesting and make some notes on why you would want to read that article. Compare it with one that you think is uninteresting.

WRITING YOUR OWN MAGAZINE ARTICLE

Look carefully at the pictures. They show things connected with Egypt which are famous.

Sphinx at Giza

Hieroglyphics, Valley of the Kings

The temple at Abu Simbel

Arab felucca boats, River Nile

Ramses II, Luxor

1 Choose one of them to write a magazine article about.

2 Research your choice and make notes on the information you will need.

3 Decide how you are going to set out your page:
   - where will the text go?
   - will you have some extra information in boxes?
   - what sort of illustrations will you have?

4 Do a rough layout of the page so you know how it is going to look.

5 Write up your article remembering to do a first draft, check it and then write a final draft.

Choose one or two of the following assignments:

1 The article on Tutankhamun gives us only part of the conversation between Lord Carnarvon and Howard Carter about having one last search for the tomb. Imagine you overheard the full conversation. What would Howard Carter have said to Lord Carnarvon to make him change his mind? Write the conversation as you imagine it might have happened.

2 Imagine you were with Howard Carter on the day he opened Tutankhamun's tomb. Write your diary entry for that day. Remember to include:
   - what happened
   - how you felt
   - how the other people with you felt.

3 According to legend, all the people who had anything to do with finding Tutankhamun's tomb died in mysterious circumstances. There are also stories of strange happenings on the day the tomb was opened. Many people say this is because of the 'curse of the Pharaohs'! Find out what you can about the mysterious deaths and strange happenings and write a report called 'The Curse of the Pharaohs'.

WORKING WITH WORDS

Howard Carter sent a **telegram** to Lord Carnarvon when he found Tutankhamun's tomb.

Tele is from Greek meaning far, or at a distance.

A **tele**gram is a message sent from a distance.

What do these **tele** words mean?

telephone   telescope   telepathy   television

Nuclear disaster!

Ann Burden is left alone after a disaster caused by a nuclear explosion. She is sixteen and believes she is the last person alive on Earth.

May 20th

I am afraid.

Someone is coming.

That is, I think someone is coming, though I am not sure, and I pray that I am wrong. I went into the church and prayed all this morning. I sprinkled water in front of the altar, and put some flowers on it, violets and dogwood.

But there is smoke. For three days there has been smoke, not like the time before. That time, last year, it rose in a great cloud a long way away, and stayed in the sky for two weeks. A forest fire in the dead woods, and then it rained and the smoke stopped. But this time it is a thin column, like a pole, not very high.

And the column has come three times, each time in the late afternoon. At night I cannot see it, and in the morning it is gone. But each afternoon it comes again, and it is nearer. At first it was behind Claypole Ridge, and I could see only the top of it, the smallest smudge. I thought it was a cloud, except that it was too grey, the wrong colour, and then I thought: there are no clouds anywhere else. I got the binoculars and saw that it was narrow and straight; it was smoke from a small fire. When we used to go in the truck, Claypole Ridge was fifteen miles, though it looks closer, and the smoke was coming from behind that.

Beyond Claypole Ridge there is Ogdentown, about ten miles further. But there is no one left alive in Ogdentown.

I know, because after the war ended, and all the telephones went dead, my father, my brother Joseph and cousin David went in the truck to find out what was happening, and the first place they went was Ogdentown. They went early in the morning; Joseph and David were really excited, but Father looked serious.

When they came back it was dark. Mother had been worrying –

they took so long – so we were glad to see the truck lights finally coming over Burden Hill, six miles away. They looked like beacons. They were the only lights anywhere, except in the house – no other cars had come down all day. We knew it was the truck because one of the lights, the left one, always blinked when it went over a bump. It came up to the house and they got out; the boys weren't excited any more. They looked scared, and my father looked sick. Maybe he was beginning to be sick, but mainly I think he was distressed.

My mother looked up at him as he climbed down.

'What did you find?'

He said, 'Bodies. Just dead bodies. They're all dead.'

'All?'

We went inside the house where the lamps were lit, the two boys following, not saying anything. My father sat down. 'Terrible,' he said, and again, 'terrible, terrible. We drove around, looking. We blew the horn. Then we went to the church and rang the bell. You can hear it five miles away. We waited for two hours, but nobody came. I went into a couple of houses – the Johnsons', the Peters' – they were all in there, all dead. There were dead birds all over the streets.'

My brother Joseph began to cry. He was fourteen. I think I had not heard him cry for six years.

From *Z for Zachariah* by Robert O'Brien

COMPREHENSION   Read the passage and answer the questions.

1 The first two sentences are an unusual opening for a story. How is the writer trying to make you feel?

2 Why does Ann think that someone is coming?

3 Why do you think she is afraid?

4 What do you think has happened to the rest of Ann's family?

5 Why do you think the people are dead, there were 'dead birds all over the streets' and Ann writes about 'dead woods'?

BOOK BLURBS

On the inside cover of a book or on the back you will find a book **blurb**. The blurb tells you a little about the story. Here is the book blurb for *Z for Zachariah*:

> LONE SURVIVOR AFTER A NUCLEAR HOLOCAUST, ANN BURDEN SEES HER SOLITARY PEACE THREATENED BY THIS UNKNOWN INTRUDER. SHE HIDES, HE WATCHES, THEY BOTH WAIT. IS HE A FRIEND AND ALLY, OR THE TERRIFYING NEAR-MANIAC SHE BEGINS TO SUSPECT? JUST AS ADAM WAS THE FIRST MAN ON EARTH, SO THIS MAN MUST BE ZACHARIAH, THE LAST . . .

Writing a book blurb is a skilled job.

- You have to let readers know enough to make them interested in reading the book.

- You must not tell readers too much so that they know what happens.

1 Write in your own words what the blurb for *Z for Zachariah* has told you.

2 What has the blurb not told?

This is a book blurb for *Little Red Riding Hood*:

> *A young girl is going to visit her old, sick grandmother. Little does she know that it is not her grandmother she will find at the cottage but someone who wishes her harm . . .*

3 Write in your own words what the blurb for *Little Red Riding Hood* has told you.

4 What has the blurb not told you?

Look at these book blurbs:

Over Sea, Under Stone by **Susan Cooper**
Like many adventures, this one began with
a holiday in Logres (land of the West and
King Arthur), the discovery of an ancient
map and a search for a buried Grail. But
then it turned into something much more
important and frightening.

The Dolphin Crossing by **Jill Paton Walsh**
Pat and his friend John both knew the risks
they were running in taking a boat across the
Channel. But they also knew they had to do
something to help the British soldiers
stranded in Dunkirk. Their story makes
intensely gripping reading.

Tom's Midnight Garden by **Philippa Pearce**
Sent to stay with his aunt and uncle in
a dull old house without even a garden,
Tom is not looking forward to his
summer holiday. However, when the
clock strikes thirteen at midnight, Tom
opens a door to find an adventure more
wonderful than he ever could have imagined.

5   Read each book blurb carefully.

6   Which blurb makes you interested enough
    to want to read the book? Why?

7   Write a book blurb for:
    a well-known children's story
    a book you have read and enjoyed recently.

8   Go to your class or school library and look at the blurbs on the
    back of some books. Pick one that interests you. Write the title
    and the author and say what it is about the blurb that makes you
    want to read the book.

Choose one or two of the following assignments:

1 Imagine you are the stranger that Ann is so afraid of in *Z for Zachariah*. You think you are the last person left alive but one day you see her from a distance. Write about how you feel and what happens at your first meeting.

2 Some people say that nuclear power is very safe. Other people think it is very dangerous. Two accidents have already occurred in nuclear power stations. One was at Three Mile Island in America and one at Chernobyl in the former USSR. Find out what you can about one of these accidents and write a report about what happened.

3 Here are the titles of some imaginary books:

Mr Morris Goes to Town
A Most Peculiar Birthday
The Strange House

Write book blurbs for two of these titles. You will have to decide what each one is about before you write your blurb.

WORKING WITH WORDS

As science progresses, it adds a lot of new words to our language. **Nuclear** energy was not known about 100 years ago.

Which of these words would you not have found in a dictionary 100 years ago?

video	gas	computer
earthquake	atom	space shuttle
camera	aspirin	fax machine